CU00825451

BILL NICHOLSON

The Master of

White Hart Lane

REVISITED

NGB

A Norman Giller Books publication

© Norman Giller 2013

First published in 2013 by NGB Publishing

Test Valley, Hampshire

A CIP catalogue for this title is available from the British Library

ISBN 978-0-9567711-2-4

Typeset and designed by NGB Publishing, Hampshire, UK

Printed and bound in the United Kingdom by CPI/Antony Rowe Ltd Bumper's Farm, Chippenham, Wiltshire SN14 6LH

Research: Michael Giller

Illustrations © 2013 Art Turner

CONTENTS

Dedicated to the memory of
Bill Nicholson
Manager supreme

KICK OFF
Norman Giller

THIS is a personal memoir of Bill Nicholson, a man and manager I was privileged to interview scores of times, and is based on the many conversations I had with him over a span of more than 40 years. My memories are boosted by an army of his old team-mates, players and fellow managers giving their eyewitness view of the achievements of one of the all-time great football philosophers and generals.

And to make it extra special, I have invited the people who mattered most to him – the Spurs supporters – to join in what is an unashamed tribute to the most loyal and influential servant in Tottenham's history.

It is not an attempt to tell the Bill Nicholson life story. That has been done more than adequately by my old Fleet Street colleague Brian Scovell (*Bill Nicholson, Football's Perfectionist, John Blake Publishing*), and Brian had earlier joined with Harry 'Scoop' Harris in ghosting Bill's own autobiography, *Glory, Glory, My Life With Spurs (Macmillan)*.

My thanks to everybody who took the trouble to join in the anthem of acclaim for the man who should by all rights have been 'Sir' William Nicholson. Thanks also to gifted artist Art Turner for his sketches that illustrate the book.

There will be a familiarity about some of the stories I tell, many of them plundered from my scrapbooks. But I do not apologise for repeating myself, because they are worth re-telling as I revisit the life and times of The Master of White Hart Lane. It is important that the young generation of Spurs fans appreciate the debt the club owes to a man who devoted his life to Tottenham Hotspur.

Now come with me back to 1958 and my introductory meeting with the new manager, Bill Nicholson ... Our story starts on the old 41 double-decker red bus that used to connect East and North London via the noisily busy North Circular Road ...

Chapter One
First impressions
of The Master

A NINEPENNY bus ride took me to my first ever meeting with Bill Nicholson. It was just before Christmas 1958 and he had been in charge at White Hart Lane for a little over eight weeks. It is part of footballing folklore how in his first game as manager Spurs had beaten Everton 10-4 in a remarkable match.

Now here I was on my way to interview him in my esteemed role as assistant sports editor of the *Stratford Express* (I had better own up here that there were only two of us on the sports staff). My meeting with 'Mr. Nicholson' had been set up for me by Vic Railton, the best connected football reporter in Fleet Street for whom I had been a dog's body copyboy and unpaid statistician for the previous two years on the London *Evening News*.

At eighteen and with the world at my feet, I was on the first rungs of the journalistic ladder, and the local football club on my reporting beat was West Ham United. They were due to play Tottenham at Upton Park on Christmas Day 1958, with the return First Division match twenty-four hours later on Boxing Day at White Hart Lane.

Mr. Nicholson had reluctantly agreed to talk to me at his cramped office at 748 Tottenham High Road, situated on the corner of an approach road to White Hart Lane that would eventually be renamed Bill Nicholson Way. It was just after lunch on the Thursday a week before the Christmas Day match, and first of all I had the challenge of trying to get past the formidable figure of Mrs Wallace, who sat in the outer office like a watchdog guarding her boss against all-comers.

She was receptionist, telephonist, ticket administrator and Nicholson's personal secretary, who protected him from the many nuisances who were a drain on his precious time. To Mrs Wallace that was anybody who tried to talk to him without an appointment noted down in her diary. My name was not there and she was just about to get rid of me like a bad smell when Mr. Nicholson appeared, fresh from a training session at the club playing fields at Cheshunt. "It's all right, Mrs W," he said. "Vic Railton set this up. You can let him in."

Mrs W reluctantly waved me through to the inner sanctum where Mr. Nicholson greeted me in a well-worn grey, woollen tracksuit that had no name or logo on it, unlike today's sponsored club kit in which managers are like walking advertising boards.

He was in grumpy mood. "I hate being in the office," he said. "It's so claustrophobic. My real office is the training ground."

No wonder. There was not room to swing a cat, a dog or a cockerel in his tiny cubicle that was located at the back of the main ticket office, with the busy high road sending in the uninvited noise and fumes of heavy traffic. Even Mrs W couldn't stop them.

He held up a fistful of letters. "Look at at all these. I've got to find the time to answer them all."

I sat uncomfortably on a hard-back chair facing him, tongue-tied and nervous at meeting a man who had been one of my heroes in his playing days that seemed just a blink of an eye ago.

He broke off from his grumbles as if suddenly realising he was being rude, reached across his desk, gripped my hand warmly and looked me straight in the eye. "You've got five minutes," he said, his Yorkshire accent watered down by nearly twenty-five years living in the south. "I'm chasing my backside. I'm only seeing you because that bloody nuisance Vic Railton nagged me into it."

An hour later we were still chatting and finally got round to talking about the West Ham games after I had pumped him for all I was worth on his days playing with the Push and Run Spurs, the side that had won my heart eight years earlier. By the end of the interview we were on 'Norman/Bill' first name terms, and bonded so well that from then on he always took my calls and granted interviews without need of dear old Vic Railton's matchmaking or the ankle-snapping from the faithful Mrs (Barbara) Wallace. Our conversations were to bridge more than 40 years.

During this first meeting with Bill I found that his passion for football in general and Spurs in particular ran as deep as the deepest ocean, as high as the highest mountain. He lived and breathed the game.

This was a first impression that never changed through the next two decades, during which I got a close-up view of the master at work but rarely at play, because he just never allowed himself leisure time. His life was football and Spurs. He, of course, found time for his charming wife, Darkie, and their two lovely daughters, Linda and Jean, but even they came second to his football calling. Bill famously cried when Linda got married because he suddenly realised he had not seen her grow up.

The reason I am focusing on my first interview with Bill is that it captures the man. Most other managers would have found an excuse to avoid having their time taken up by a young, nobody reporter. But he, beneath the gruff exterior, was warm and kind-hearted and could not bring himself to tell me to get lost. I never ever knew Bill be anything but a thorough gentleman; often a moaner and a groaner but never less than polite.

At this first meeting, I think he was surprised by my knowledge of Spurs. More like a starry-eyed fan than a professional reporter, I drew from him the following pearls that I pass on to strengthen your familiarity with that wonderful Push and Run Spurs side in which Bill Nick played a key role as a functional and thoughtful right-half:

How vital was Arthur Rowe to that team? "He was the architect of the system. Remember that he won the Second and First Division championships in back to back seasons with virtually the same players he had inherited from Joe Hulme. That was down to Arthur's organisational and coaching skills. He believed, like me, in keeping things simple. Make it simple, make it quick. When not in possession, get into position. Give it, and go. Arthur was full of these sort of easy to remember instructions, and I use many of them with my players today."

Who was the most influential player in the side? "We were very much a team and we had no prima donnas or selfish individualists. Our motto was the same as the Musketeers, all for one and one for all. I doubt if we could have been so successful without the measured passes of Eddie Baily, but for me the player who had the biggest influence was our skipper Ronnie Burgess. We joined Spurs the same week in the 1930s and grew up together with the same standards and discipline. He was a powerhouse of a player who could be driving the attack forward one minute and then back clearing and tackling in defence the next. Ron made the rest of us lift our game and our energy to try to keep up with him."

If you could turn back the clock, which of the forwards would you like to score goals for you today? "It would have to be the Duke, Len Duquemin. He was raw when he first arrived from the Channel Islands but developed a good positional sense and had a cannonball shot. Len was lucky to be served by two outstanding wingers in Sonny Walters and Les Medley, and he and Les Bennett struck up a radar-like understanding of where to be to get the best out of each other. They were a real handful in our championship season."

Were you disappointed not to get more than your one cap, while Alf Ramsey got 32? "Not at all. Billy Wright played in my position and was a better player. Simple as that. I used to pull Alf's leg and tell him that he got so many caps because of all the running I did to cover for him. He was a magnificent defender with great vision. His distribution was an important part of our success. He is now a fine manager with Ipswich Town. They will be worth watching because Alf has got a lot of good ideas that, like me, he picked up under Arthur Rowe. He is very inventive with his tactical thoughts. That's why we used to call him The General."

Why was the Push and Run era over so quickly? "Well I like to think we're continuing it. Our style is not dissimilar to how we used to play under Arthur. A bit quicker, but the principles are the same. You have to remember that most of the Push and Run players came through wartime military service that robbed us of five or more years. Many of us were past our peak by the time we won the Championship. Now my hope is to be able to put together a team that is nearly as good."

The players union is pressing for the abolition of the maximum wage. Do you agree it should be kicked out? "I don't know what the players union is on about. If you can't live on £20 a week there's something wrong with your housekeeping. Money should never be the motivation for players. The thing that should drive them is pride in their performances and a love for the game. I would willingly have played for nothing, just as long as I was enjoying my football. Too much money in the game will just cause problems, in my opinion. But I don't suppose too many players will agree with me. I don't like greed in any shape or form."

Our chat was interrupted by veteran trainer Cecil Poynton popping his head around the door of Bill's office, not seeing me and saying in his West Midlands accent: "Alfie's playing up again, Bill. If he gave as much attention to his training as he does to following the dogs he'd be a much better and fitter player. He lost a packet again last night and is on the scrounge."

Bill pointed to me. "Got company at the moment, Cec," he said, giving me a quick introduction. "This is your test young man. If I read one word of what Cecil has just said about Alfie Stokes you will never again get an interview with me or any of my staff."

I would never have dreamed of reporting what I had accidentally overheard. Alfie was notorious in the game for his gambling, and as far as I was concerned it was a private matter between him and the club

For some reason, Cecil felt he should add to my education. "Young feller," he said, "you'll find many of today's footballers are more interested in talking about shagging than football. You press people have a duty to make them take the game more seriously. I can't understand them. I'm at the age when I'd much rather have a good shit than a shag." (It took me another 50-plus years to understand what he meant).

With that profound parting shot, Cecil left us to our chat, Bill putting a hand to his wide, freckled forehead as he watched the departing figure of Poynton. "Dear old Cecil," he said, with a mixture of warmth and wonderment. "He's been here so long he's part of the furniture. We always encourage loyalty and long service at Spurs. We're like one big, happy family."

Before Bill finally got rid of me, he said how much he was looking forward to the back-to-back matches against West Ham the following week. "They have good footballing traditions," he said. "I think they'll be attractive games to watch, and we're confident of getting more than a share of the points."

In fact Hammers had the happier Christmas, winning 2-1 at Upton Park and by a thumping 4-1 at the Lane, no doubt helping the rush of Bill's gingery hair to a steel grey. Alfie Stokes played in both games, but before the season was much older he had been sold to Fulham. Harringay Greyhound Track bookmakers were rumoured to have wept at the news of his transfer.

Spurs finished an uncomfortable 18th in the First Division table, but Bill Nick was rebuilding – dare I say, at the double!

Bill had listened with the patience of a schoolteacher hearing a gushing young pupil talk about his discovery of ice cream as I bored him with the background to my admiration – now an addiction – for Spurs. So that you can more easily understand that first flush of excitement let me share with you an article I wrote for the Spurs' Writers' Club book, *Glory Glory Tottenham Hotspur*. I hope it makes you reach for your own memories of when you first fell in love with the club:

THE classic opening words to *The Go Between* by English novelist L. P. Hartley could have been written with the whirling world of football in mind: "The past is a foreign country … they do things differently there."

Here we are in the 1950-51 season. The place The Valley, the match Charlton Athletic v. Tottenham Hotspur, and there I am – a skinny as a pipe cleaner ten-year-old primary schoolboy in my older brother's hand-me-down short trousers – trembling with excitement and anticipation of my first view of First Division football. I had been taken south of the Thames from my East End home by my Uncle Roy Robinson, who was expecting to convert me to his religion of worshipping Charlton.

It was a different game then, not just another country but another planet. Rationbook times, London still being rebuilt after the Second World War blitz, footballers earning £11 a week, going to and from the ground like the rest of us by bus and speaking a language that would be foreign to today's players.

There were wing-halves, inside-forwards, shoulder-charging and barging of goalkeepers, tackling from behind, two points for a win, no floodlights, no yellow and red cards, no TV cameras, a leather and laced panelled ball that was like a pudding on heavy, mud-heap pitches that made every step a challenge.

This trip to The Valley of dreams cost my Uncle three shillings (15p), two bob for him and a shilling (5p) for me to stand on the vast, concrete terracing behind the goal at the Floyd Road end of the sprawling stadium. There were 62,000 spectators shoehorned into the ground, and I could not see a thing through the heaving wall of fans towering above me.

No problem. Dock worker Uncle Roy picked me up as if I was a packing case and handed me high to the man in front, and I was carried on a willing relay of raised hands above hundreds of heads, most adorned with flat caps, and down to a cramped standing place against the fence, right behind the goal being defended by Tottenham.

I will not pretend that sixty-plus years on I can remember the exact details of the match, but what has remained with me is the sense of excitement and the sheer ecstasy of feeling as if I was involved in the action. Yes, a spectator but I kicked every ball, scored goals that were missed and made every save. All these years later that sense of involvement in every game has never left me.

I have been the Stanley Matthews, the Pele, the Bobby Charlton, the Greavsie, the Glenn Hoddle, the Gareth Bale of spectators. If

Ted Ditchburn, daring and defiant last line of defence for the Push and Run Spurs. When I saw him, it was love at first flight.

13

only they would play the game the way I see it, my team would never lose

My Uncle Roy had been teaching me chants: "Come on you Robins ..." ... "Get in there you 'Addicks.'" He wanted me to wear a red and white rosette as big as my head, but instinct made me declare myself too shy to pin it to my jacket.

Little did he know that I had been nobbled before he got to me by another uncle, Eddie Baldwin of Edmonton, who was my Godfather. He and my Aunt Emmy were Spurs through and through, and followed them home and away. The home bit was easy. They lived within the crowd's roar of White Hart Lane.

They had been filling my head and my imagination with stories of the great Tottenham teams, and telling me how they had waltzed away with the Second Division title in 1949-50 with what was known as Push and Run football. The cynics sneered that it was playground football that would be exposed in the top echelon of the First Division.

Now here I was immediately behind the goal at The Valley watching Arthur Rowe's Spurs chase and chastise Charlton with their push and run tactics that were simple yet sophisticated, predictable yet played to perfection. They followed the Arthur Rowe commandments: "When not in possession get into position ... make it simple, make it quick ... keep the ball on the ground ... the three As, accuracy, accuracy, accuracy ..."

There at right-back Alf Ramsey was showing the poise and polish that made him a regular in the England team. Ahead of him right-half Billy (that's what they called him then) Nicholson, gingery-haired, full of energy and urgency, making the team tick with his unselfish running and tigerish tackling. Striding across the pitch like a colossus was skipper Ronnie Burgess, as tough as if hewn from a Welsh mountain but able to intersperse delicate skill with his startling strength (no wonder Bill Nicholson once described him to me as the greatest player ever to pull on a Spurs shirt). Burgess would prompt the attack, and then in a blink of an eye be back at the heart of the defence helping out alongside immense centre-half Harry Clarke.

Imperious in the centre of the pitch was the thick-thighed emperor of the team, Eddie Baily, the 'Cheeky Chappie' of the dressing-room who could land a ball on a flannel from forty yards. He was the schemer-in-chief, providing a conveyor belt of telling passes for twin centre-forwards Len 'The Duke' Duquemin and Londoner Les Bennett. The Duke was a Channel Islander, the nearest thing to a 'foreigner' on the Spurs books.

Tottenham's alternative route to goal was down the wings, with flying Sonny Walters and tricky Les Medley turning defences inside out with their stunning running. Their crosses, usually to the far post, were met high and mightily by the Duke or Bennett, both of whom could head the ball as hard as I could kick it.

Incredibly, fifteen or so years later, I would be regularly interviewing Alf, Bill Nick, Ron Burgess and Eddie Baily in my role as chief football reporter for the *Daily Express*. Seeing them through my schoolboy eyes they were like giants, but one player stood above them all.

In about the tenth minute of the match, Charlton's South African centre-forward Stuart Leary – an outstanding cricketer with Kent – took aim with a thunderbolt shot from the edge of the Tottenham penalty area.

From my best view in the ground, I could see that the ball was going to fly into the top right hand corner of the net. Fifty thousand of the 62,000 crowd – Charlton fans – roared in anticipation of a goal and hundreds of wooden rattles produced an ear-shattering background effect like a snarl of snare drums.

Then, seemingly from out of nowhere, appeared somebody doing a Superman impression. Was it a bird,was it a plane? No, it was the flying form of goalkeeper Ted Ditchburn, not touching the ball away like most goalkeepers would have tried to do. My schoolboy eyes looked on in amazement as he caught it while at full stretch and in mid-air.

It was a stunning, astonishing save that silenced everybody but the knot of 12,000 travelling Tottenham fans at the other end of the ground, who switched from cheering to choruses of the club theme song, McNamara's Band.

From that moment on I was a Tottenham disciple. It was love at first flight.

Throughout a long football reporting career I had to stick to press box neutrality, and it is not until recently surrendering newspaper work for full-time authorship that I have been able to come out of the closet as a Spurs supporter. And I can trace the start of my love affair to that magical moment when Ted Ditchburn appeared to defy gravity and make a save that has lived on in my memory.

Thank goodness there were no television action replays to taint or tarnish the picture in my head. It still sits there, and is occasionally brought out from the vaults of my memory and admired, without anybody being able to produce proof that perhaps, just perhaps, I have exaggerated the lightning shaft of genius that turned me into a lover of all things Lilywhite.

For the record, Spurs forced a 1-1 draw thanks to an Alf Ramsey penalty and they pushed and ran their way to the League championship.

There was controversy when Charlton celebrated what they thought was a winning goal from a powerfully driven free-kick by Syd O'Lynn. The ball flashed past my new hero Ditchburn into the corner of the net, but the victory roars died in Charlton throats when the referee ordered the free-kick to be re-taken because the Spurs defensive wall was not ten yards back. Charlton argued, with some justification, that they had been punished for Tottenham breaking the rules.

The relieved Spurs supporters danced with delight and broke into choruses of McNamara's Band, with words known like a litany by true Tottenham fans ... and not a mention of the 'Y' word.

And a ten-year-old boy in his brother's hand me down short trousers went home to the East End converted to the Tottenham way of playing football.

Now, back to revisiting Bill Nicholson, after a quick, sing-along burst of McNamara's Band ....

McNamara's Band was adopted by the Spurs' Supporters Club in the late 1940s, based on the song popularised by Bing Crosby:

We are Spurs supporters and we love to watch them play
We go to all the home games, and we go to those away
With us supporters following them, we know they'll do all right
We loudly cheer when they appear, the lads in blue and white

We're proud of our football ground, it's known throughout the land
And while we wait for the game to start we listen to the band
And when we see the teams come out you should hear the roar
We know it won't be long before the Spurs they start to score

The ref his whistle proudly blows, the linesmen wave their flags
The Duke is ready to kick off as he hitches up his bags
We cheer Sonny Walters as he toddles down the line
And the ball like magic is in the net and makes us all feel fine

There's Ronnie Burgess with his skill holding up the line
With Alf, Bill, Harry and Charlie way up there behind
And not forgetting dear old Ted whose hands are sure and strong
And Eddie and the Leslies who are always up-along

And when the game is over, when the game is through
We cheer the winners off the field and the gallant losers too
The cockerel proudly wags his tail, he gave Spurs their name
In honour of the Lilywhites who always play the game

Now come on all you supporters and join our merry band
No matter what your age is, we'll take you by the hand
We'll pin a cockerel on your chest, it shows the world that we
Are members of that loyal band, the S-S-C.

Chapter Two
The Great Coach Journey

ABOVE all things, Bill considered himself a coach. Managing came as an accident, while coaching was always a driving force. As I learned from my first meeting with him he hated being stuck in his office doing managerial duties. He became six inches taller the moment he stepped on to the training pitch and started spreading his football gospel. Here, everybody understood his language and there were no boring boardroom politics or time-consuming correspondence to bother him. The training ground was where he came alive. Ask any player coached by Bill Nick and they will tell you how lucky they were to have listened and learned at the great man's feet.

Back in the 1960s I went to a coaching conference at the FA training centre on the lush playing fields of Lilleshall in Shropshire. I drove up from London with my close friend Dave Sexton, who was just starting his managing career with Leyton Orient. We had a mutual love of boxing and jazz as our common ground, but it was football that ate up most of Dave's sleeping and waking time. He was a fanatic. Dave admired Bill to the point of hero worship, and told me how he wanted his Orient team to play the Spurs way.

"Bill represents football with dignity and style," Dave said. "His teams are always positive and a joy to watch. He is proving himself one of the finest managers the game has ever seen, but more than that he is an exceptional coach and fine person."

Nick was the main speaker at the conference and got such a warm reception that for a moment he was lost for words. He had recently followed the Double by capturing the FA Cup again and then the European Cup Winners' Cup, but he was such a modest man that he had no idea how highly he was regarded by his peers.

He had been one of the first to come through the FA coaching courses set up in the immediate post-war years by the father of coaching, Walter Winterbottom, and before that he had been hugely influenced by renowned athletics coach Geoff Dyson, who convinced him during their wartime work together as PTIs that physical fitness mattered as much as basic skill.

"It doesn't matter how talented a footballer you are," Bill said, "if you are not 100 per cent physically fit you will get found out. This is why at Tottenham we have a pre-season fitness programme that is like an assault course. Many of the players hate it, but they know it will serve them well as a grounding for the challenges ahead. You will never find Tottenham players hiding in a match while they try to catch their breath. If they do hide, I will want to know why."

At the time of the Lilleshall conference there was concern at the lack of skill among the young players coming to clubs for trials (nothing changes). During his address to the coaches Bill made a point that will strike a chord with readers of a certain age:

●I wish we could go back to the days when parents gave their boys a tanner ball for their Christmas and birthday presents. Young footballers of my generation never went anywhere without that small ball at their feet. The youngsters who come for trials today have nothing like as good control of the ball as we did. They need two or three touches before they can get it under control, and it is rare these days to find a two-footed player. I don't think we should be encouraging ball hoggers but I do believe we should be working at schools level to get the boys feeling comfortable with a ball at their feet. I bet if you go to Jimmy Greaves, Bobby Charlton, Johnny Haynes, or Denis Law they will tell you they always had a tanner ball to dribble in front of them when they were kids. Let's get back to basics.●

Bill was so outstanding on the FA coaching courses that England manager Walter Winterbottom selected him as his right hand man for the World Cup challenge in Sweden in 1958. It is part of the Nicholson legend how Bill went to watch eventual champions Brazil play and came up with the tactics that produced a creditable 0-0 draw against the Pele-propelled team that was slaughtering all opposition.

This is what Winterbottom, literally a gentleman and a scholar, a former schoolteacher, told me:

•I had my hands full with our match against Russia, and so asked Bill to check out Brazil against Austria. He came back with a notebook full of assessments of every player, their overall tactics and just about everything you could possibly want to know about a team. It was remarkable in its thoroughness and observation. Working to Bill's analysis, we staged a practice match with Bill and I joining in as pretend Brazilians against our first-choice team. We demonstrated the positions they took at set pieces, and Bill gave concise instructions as to how to cramp the space for their forwards. I wish I had saved the notes as an example of the perfect in-depth reconnaissance. That goalless draw against the magnificent Brazilians was one of the highlights of my career as England team manager, and there is no question that Bill Nicholson should take much of the credit.•

I tried hard to draw Bill on his part in that plotting against Brazil, arguably the greatest international team of all time. But he just shrugged and said, "I only did my job. It was a privilege to help Walter, one of the finest coaches there has ever been."

That was typical Bill, shifting the praise to somebody else. There were times when I wanted to kick him for not taking his deserved role at centre stage, but then it would not have been the Bill Nick we all grew to admire, respect and – yes – love.

SCRAPBOOK MEMORIES: Bill signed my scrapbook for me back in the 1960s and told me a fascinating story about this photo

He was one of the few football people whose autograph I ever requested. I asked him to sign the photograph featured in this chapter that was in a 1950s coaching book. Bill winced when he saw the photograph.

"Ouch," he said. "That brings back painful memories. I was having awful problems with my right knee. You can see I have an elastic bandage on it. I might look in complete command there but even posing for that photograph sent a pain shooting through my knee. Shortly after that my knee seized up altogether, and I had to have an operation and was hobbling on sticks for quite a while. It made me realise that I was never going to get back to my peak form and fitness and I decided it was best for the club and the team if I retired."

The Push and Run team was breaking up, most of them World War Two veterans who had seen the best years of their careers lost to six years of war.

Bill recalled:

•Eddie Baily, Alf Ramsey and I were all photographed that day. It was for a coaching book that had the blessing of the FA. But by the time the book was published not one of us was playing for Spurs anymore. Alf had moved on to Ipswich, Eddie to Port Vale and me into coaching. It was also about that time that Arthur Rowe had health problems and had to stand down. Jimmy Anderson took over in a caretaker role and invited me to be his coach. Then Arthur came back for a short while until he could not carry on anymore, and Jimmy was then officially manager. Arthur Rowe's Push and Run era was over. They were great days, in many ways the best of my life. You can't beat playing. But then I poured myself into coaching, and trying to pass on to players all the good habits I had learned with Arthur and Walter. I had no designs on the manager's job. I just wanted to coach. It was what I liked doing best.•

As well as the skill aspect, Bill was always pushing the three

F's to his players during training, and the most vital 'f' word in his vocabulary was Fitness ... Fitness ... Fitness. He once told me: "D'you know which are the fittest athletes in the world? Ballet dancers! Yes, they are supreme athletes. I remember once on a pre-season club tour of Russia in 1959 we went to the Bolshoi Ballet in Moscow. Most of the lads grumbled when I told them what we were going to see, but they came away astonished at the fitness and stamina of those dancers. I got our interpreter to ask questions back stage and I found they did lots of controlled weight training for muscle development, and so I invited an Olympic weightlifter called Bill Watson to introduce weight training into our fitness programme. It made a huge difference to our fitness levels."

Only Bill could have sat watching the Bolshoi and seen athletes rather than ballet dancers!

At the instigation of Walter Winterbottom, he coupled coaching at Spurs with taking charge of the Cambridge University team. Their rivals in the annual Varsity match were Oxford, coached by Bill's friend and former Tottenham team-mate Vic Buckingham.

Despite all the brain power – on the pitch and on the bench – the two teams could only manage a goalless draw in their one meeting under the batons of the two Tottenham footballing professors.

"Something I learned from that experience," said Bill, "is that intellectual powers do not translate to football ability on the pitch. Some of the greatest footballers I worked with over the years had low IQs, while many of the brilliant academics I coached at Cambridge could not trap a bag of cement. If brains and intelligence counted that much you would have university educated people dominating our football. It just doesn't happen."

But a player had just arrived at White Hart Lane to take over Bill's No 4 shirt who was to prove that intellectuals could play with style and guile.

This was Danny Blanchflower, who had the gift of the gab and educated feet.

Chapter Three
Ten Goals,
Just for Starters

NOBODY can give an accurate account of Bill Nicholson's glory-glory adventures at Tottenham without shining a light on his astonishing first match in charge. Few managers in the history of the Beautiful Game have had such a startling start to a career.

On the morning of Saturday October 11 1958 – a date that should be carved into Tottenham hearts – Bill Nicholson was officially promoted from coach to manager in succession to the fatigued Jimmy Anderson.

In the afternoon his team treated him to a banquet that left even the hungriest spectators completely gorged. Providing the opposition were Everton, who were struggling three from the bottom of the First Division, a point behind sixteenth-placed Spurs.

The first decision Nicholson made in his new role was to recall Tottenham's impish inside-forward Tommy Harmer, known to the White Hart Lane fans as 'Harmer the Charmer.' But that afternoon Everton found him more like 'The Harmer' as he pulled them apart with an astounding individual performance. He had a hand – or rather a well-directed foot – in nine goals and scored one himself as Everton were sunk without trace under a flood of goals. The final scoreline was 10-4. It could just easily have been 15-8!

Harmer was the 'Tom Thumb' character of football. He stood just 5ft 2in tall and was a chain-smoking bantamweight who looked as if he could be blown away by a strong wind. But he had mesmeric control of the ball and when conditions suited him could dominate a match with his passing and dribbling.

Born in Hackney on February 2 1928, he joined Tottenham from amateur club Finchley in 1951 and over the next eight years played 205 League games and scored 47 goals.

For the record, Bill Nicholson's first selection as Spurs manager:

Hollowbread, Baker, Hopkins, Blanchflower, Ryden, Iley, Medwin, Harmer, Smith, Stokes, Robb.

There was a hint of what was to come in the opening moments when Spurs took the lead through Alfie Stokes after an inch-perfect diagonal pass from Harmer had split the Everton defence. The Merseysiders steadied themselves and equalised eight minutes later when Jimmy Harris side footed in a Dave Hickson centre.

The unfortunate Albert Dunlop, deputising in goal for the injured first-choice 'keeper Jimmy O'Neill, then suffered a nightmare thirty minutes as Spurs ruthlessly smashed five goals past him through skipper Bobby Smith (2), schoolmaster George Robb, Stokes again and Terry Medwin.

The foundation for all the goals was being laid in midfield where Harmer and Danny Blanchflower, both masters of ball control, were in complete command.

Jimmy Harris gave Everton fleeting hope of a revival with a headed goal to make it 6-2 just after half-time, but bulldozing Bobby Smith took his personal haul to four and the irrepressible Harmer helped himself to a goal that was as spectacular as any scored during this gourmet feast.

Bobby Collins lost possession just outside the penalty area, and the ball bobbled in front of Harmer. He struck it on the half volley from twenty yards and watched almost in disbelief as the ball rocketed into the roof of the net. It was the first time Tommy had scored a League goal from outside the penalty area.

Everton refused to surrender and the industrious Harris completed his hat-trick from a centre by dashing centre-forward Dave Hickson. Then Bobby Collins, just an inch taller than Harmer, showed that this was a magical match for the wee people when he hammered in a 25-yard drive as both teams crazily pushed everybody forward. It was like watching two hard-hitting heavyweight boxers with fragile chins slugging it out.

All the goals were scored by forwards until Spurs centre-half John Ryden, limping on the wing, scrambled in Tottenham's tenth goal – the fourteenth of the match – in the closing minutes. Bill Nick, finding it hard to believe what he had witnessed, was close to speechless. It was years later when he told me:

•I've never believed in fairy tales in football, but this came close to making me change my mind. In many ways it was a bad advertisement for football because so many of the goals were the result of slip-shod defensive play. But I have to admit it was magnificent entertainment. Little Tommy Harmer played the game of his life. On his day he was as clever a player as I've ever seen, but he was too often handicapped by his small physique. When I went to the ground that day I had a good idea I'd be taking charge because the chairman had told me in the week that Jimmy was unwell and wanted to know if I would consider taking over as manager. The chairman called me into the boardroom and confirmed my appointment. I did not ask for a contract. I just agreed to take over and later in the day came the amazing game with Everton.•

Jimmy Harris commented:

•It was a good news, bad news day for me. I was able to tell people that I had scored a hat-trick against Spurs, and would then mumble the bad news that we had lost 10-4. It's no exaggeration to say we could have had at least four more goals. I don't know who were the more bewildered by it all – the players or the spectators, who got tremendous value for their money. Tommy Harmer was the man who won it for Tottenham. It was as if he had the ball on a piece of string and he continually pulled our defence apart with clever runs and probing passes.•

Tuppence would have bought you the match day programme for Bill Nicholson's first game as manager ... with J. Anderson still listed as the team manager.

Hero Harmer said:

•I had been out of the League team for the previous four matches and was half expecting to be left out again when I reported for the match with Everton. But Bill Nick told me I was in, and it became one of those games when just everything went right for me. I particularly remember my goal because it was about the only time I ever scored from that sort of range.•

As Tommy came off the pitch to a standing ovation, he said to Bill Nicholson: "I hope you're not going to expect ten goals from us every week, Boss!"

Danny Blanchflower was even more pessimistic, but with his Irish tongue firmly in his cheek. "We can only go downhill from here," he said. "How do you follow ten goals? Things can only get worse."

The astonishing thing is that Bill did not tell his wife, Darkie, that he was being promoted to manager. "I never used to take business home with me," Bill explained. "I was eaten up with thinking about tactics and which team to pick. Never had time for tittle tattle."

Yes, Bill had tunnel vision but he could always see the bright light of a successful team at the end of it. The thought of winning games with style is what drove him. And he wanted to do it all with a minimum of fuss.

Only three players from the Spurs team that scored the knock-out ten goals survived as regular members of the Double-winning side of 1960-61– right-back Peter Baker, artistic right-half Danny Blanchflower and centre-forward Bobby Smith. The fourteen goals equalled the aggregate First Division record set in 1892 when Aston Villa annihilated Accrington Stanley 12-2.

This was just the start for The Team That Bill Built. The Glory-Glory days were around the corner.

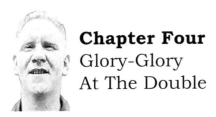

Chapter Four
Glory-Glory
At The Double

WITHIN two years of my first wide-eyed meeting with Bill Nick, he had pieced together one of the most formidable teams ever to grace the playing fields of England. You cannot revisit his life and times without quickly bringing the astonishing exploits of the 1960-61 season to the surface.

This was what Bill told me about that Double team in a moment of rosy reflection:

•Everything was right. The balance of the team. The attitude of the players. We managed to find the perfect blend and everybody gave 100 per cent in effort and enthusiasm. We had the sort of understanding and cohesion that you find in only the finest teams, and we tried to keep our football as simple as possible – imaginative but simple. I kept pushing an old theory: 'When you're not in possession, get into position.' The man *without* the ball was important, because he could make things happen by getting into the right place at the right time. Running off the ball was as vital as running with it. The secret is finding space and using it.•

His greatest strength as a manager was his tactical under-standing of a game that he always believed should be kept simple. Remember, he had been heavily influenced by first Peter McWilliam in the 1930s and then Arthur Rowe in the 1940s/50s, both exceptional Tottenham managers. While too many coaches were trying to turn football into a sort of master-class chess, he kept it simple yet sophisticated His teams played football that was easy to understand and beautiful to watch. And it was also stunningly effective. The Nicholson record speaks for itself:

League and FA Cup double (1960-61)

FA Cup (1961, 1962 and 1967)

European Cup Winners' Cup (1963)

Uefa Cup (1972)

League Cup (1971 and 1973)

FA Charity Shield: 1961, 1962, shared 1967

But in a way it was all downhill after the Double Year. He was like a man who had fallen in love with the most beautiful girl in the world, and spent the rest of his years trying to find an exact copy. He never quite managed to recreate a team on a par with the 'Super Spurs' of 1960-61.

For those not lucky to have been around to witness the feats of those Double heroes, let me try to paint a retrospective picture, hopefully warming the memories of those of a certain age who were there to enjoy the magical moments.

For a start, Nicholson's Double team was never defence minded – as is revealed by the fact that they conceded 50 League goals on their way to the First Division championship. But they were sufficiently steady at the back to allow heavy concentration on attack. Goalkeeper Bill Brown, one of the more efficient Scottish goalkeepers, had excellent reactions and a safe pair of hands, which made up for his occasional positioning misjudgment. He had a good rapport with the 6 foot 1 inch Norfolk-born giant Maurice Norman, a dominating centre-half who won 23 England caps. He was flanked in a fluid 3-3-4 formation by full-backs Peter Baker and Ron Henry, both of whom were disciplined and determined and had unyielding competitive attitudes.

Dave Mackay was always quick to take up a defensive position

SCRAPBOOK MEMORIES: Bill Nick in a rare moment of showing off in the Tottenham trophy room. I set up this photo for my Daily Express colleague Norman Quicke in 1973, in the week of the Spurs League Cup final victory over Norwich at Wembley. Another pot for Bill!

alongside Norman when needed and his tackles were like a clap of thunder. They used to say in the game that anybody who felt the full weight of a Mackay challenge would go home feeling as if he was still with them. Danny Blanchflower was not noted for his tackling but was a shrewd enough positional player to manage to get himself between the opponent in possession and the goal. He would defend with the instincts of a sheepdog, cornering the opposition by steering them into cul-de-sacs rather than biting them. He left that to the Great Mackay.

The Tottenham attacking movements in that Double year were full of fluency and fire, a blaze lit in midfield by three of the greatest players to come together in one club team (up there with Best-Law-and-Charlton and Moore-Hurst-Peters). Blanchflower, an inspiring skipper for Northern Ireland as well as Tottenham, was the brains of the team who had an instinctive feel for the game and an ability to lift the players around him with measured passes and intelligent tactical commands.

He was the sort of confident captain who would sort things out on the pitch in the heat of battle rather than wait until the after-match dressing-room inquest.

This was not understood or welcomed by Bill Nicholson's predecessor Jimmy Anderson, who fell out with Danny and dropped him after he had switched tactics in the losing 1956 FA Cup semi-final against Manchester City. Danny had the last laugh after a frustrating spell in the reserves.

Mackay, the Scot with an in-built swagger and a he-man's barrel chest, was the heart of the side, always playing with enormous enthusiasm, power and panache, and a creative left foot.

John White, an artist of an inside-forward in the best traditions of purist Scottish football, was the eyes of the team, seeing openings that escaped the vision of lesser players and dismantling defences with precision passes and blind-side runs that earned him the nickname, 'The Ghost of White Hart Lane'. This talented trio were essentially buccaneering, forward-propelling players, but were sufficiently geared to team discipline to help out in defence when necessary.

Spearheading the attack in that memorable start to the swinging 'sixties was burly, bulldozing centre-forward Bobby Smith, a 15-cap England centre-forward who mixed subtle skill with awesome strength. He was the main marksman in the Double year with 33 League and Cup goals.

The mighty Smith was in harness with Les Allen, father of future Spurs hero Clive. He was a clever and under-rated player who was the odd man out when Jimmy Greaves arrived the following season. Les contributed 23 goals to the championship season. Smith, Allen and Greaves all started their careers with Chelsea.

Out on the wings Spurs had Terry Dyson – tiny, quick and taunting, the son of a Yorkshire jockey – and the marvellous Cliff Jones, one of the 'Untouchables' of Welsh international football, who could take the tightest defences apart with his fast, diagonal runs. In reserve Spurs had players of the calibre of Welsh terrier Terry Medwin, fearless Frank Saul, cultured wing-half Tony Marchi and utility player John Smith, all of whom made occasional appearances during that golden season.

Spurs set a new First Division record by winning their opening eleven matches on the trot (or more at a smooth canter). Blanchflower found his was no longer a voice in the wilderness. Good judges began to wonder if – as Danny had been insisting from day one – this could be the year for the Double. Spurs were looking that good.

Aston Villa were crushed by six goals, Manchester United by four, and mighty Wolves were hammered by four goals on their own territory at Molineux. They were victories that brought gasps of astonishment and admiration right around the country, because Man United and Wolves were still living on their reputations of the previous decade of being the kings of English football.

It was records all the way as Tottenham romped to the League championship with eight points to spare over runners-up Sheffield Wednesday. Their 31 victories constituted a League record, as did their total of sixteen away wins. The 66 points collected with style and flamboyance equalled the First Division record set by Herbert Chapman's Arsenal in 1930-31.

While winning the First Division marathon they also managed to survive in the minefield of the FA Cup, getting a scare in the sixth round at Sunderland, but winning the replay 6-0 at White Hart Lane.

The Final against a Leicester City team handicapped by injury problems was something of an anti-climax, but Spurs managed to win 2-0 to prove Danny Blanchflower as good a prophet as he was a footballing captain. Bobby Smith and Terry Dyson scored the victory-clinching goals past the goalkeeper who was to become a legend, Gordon Banks.

On the way to the League title, all five of Tottenham's first-choice goal-hunting forwards reached double figures – Bobby Smith (28), Les Allen (23), Cliff Jones (15), John White (13) and Terry Dyson (12).

These were the twelve men who carried off the League championship and FA Cup trophies in a style that was almost poetical:

Brown, Baker, Henry
They roll off the tongue like old friends
Blanchflower, Norman, Mackay
Creating a legend that never ends
Jones, White, Smith
They played the game with style and flair
Allen, Dyson, Medwin
And were – at the double – beyond compare

Most poetical of all was skipper Danny Blanchflower, who became a colleague of mine on *Express* newspapers when he seamlessly followed playing the game with writing about it. He told me:

•When I predicted to our chairman before the start of the season that we would achieve the double I said it quietly and confidently ... but not confidentially, because I wanted to get the message out. It was not a boast but a belief. I am a great believer that confidence, like fear, can be contagious, and I wanted our players to catch my belief. It was a question of making everybody at the club think not 'we may' but 'we can'. It was positive thinking to go with our positive play.

"I was impressed by the individual ability running through our squad, also its teamwork, and its whole personality. You could say we were one of the last of the good teams in which players were allowed to do things their own way, without restrictions from the coaching manual. Bill Nicholson deserves enormous respect and praise for the way he ran our ship. He was a captain who knew when to stay on the bridge, but also when to come and mix with the men and inspire and motivate them with good commonsense tactics. He is an absolute master of a coach who knows how to get his ideas across without being confusing or complicated. Football is basically a simple game that is sometimes made more complicated than it need be by the people doing the coaching. Bill Nicholson made us do the basics well but gave the freedom to think for ourselves.

"I sensed people grew to like us because we were a cosmopolitan team as well as a very good one. We had Englishmen, Welshmen, Scots and Irishmen, big guys, little guys, fat men and thin men. Also, we scored goals in so many different ways. I know if I had been a spectator I would have wanted to watch us. We were exciting, explosive and – virtually throughout the season – exceptional.'

In 1982, I had the assignment of scripting the centenary tribute Spurs video (*100 Years of Spurs*), which was presented by Jimmy Greaves and the first official video released featuring the club's rich history. By then, Bill Nick was employed at Tottenham in a scouting and consultancy role, and Jimmy and I sat him down and got this man by man assessment of the Double team (I've added the stats):

BILL BROWN

Born Dundee October 8 1931. Tottenham goalkeeper in 222 League matches between 1959 and 1965 after joining them from his local Dundee club during Bill Nicholson's first season as manager. He was capped 28 times by Scotland, and wound down his League career with Northampton Town. Throughout his career he worked part-time on building up a printing business, eventually emigrating to Canada where he he went into real estate after briefly playing for Toronto Falcons. Bill passed on in 2004.

BILL NICK APPRAISAL: "I was faced with the huge problem of finding a successor to Ted Ditchburn, who had been one of the finest goalkeepers in the country when playing for us. My Scottish contacts tipped me off that Dundee were willing to listen to offers for Bill, who was the current Scotland goalkeeper and I jumped on the overnight train to Dundee in the 1959 close season and snapped him up for £16,500. He had a good pair of hands, was very agile, and stood his ground when aggressive forwards tried to unsettle him. He quickly established a good rapport with centre-half Maurice Norman, and between them they usually managed to clear any danger. There were sometimes questions about his ability to deal with crosses but he rarely let Spurs down. I would rate him one of my most important and successful signings, and he continued to do a fine job for us while we waited for Pat Jennings to settle."

PETER BAKER

Born Hampstead, London, December 10 1931. Played 299 League games for Spurs, and scored three goals. Signed for Tottenham from Enfield in 1952 at the age of 20, during the Arthur Rowe era and served the club for nearly 14 years. After eventually losing his place in defence to Cyril Knowles (who was more comfortable on the left), he wound down his career in South Africa with Durban City. Educated in Arsenal territory at Southgate County School, he was the only player in the Double defence not to win an international cap.

BILL NICK APPRAISAL: "Peter was an established member of the staff when I took over, and I had great confidence in him because he was an excellent all-round sportsman with good stamina and an impressive fitness level. His hard, uncompromising style balanced perfectly with the more skilled approach of his partner Ron Henry. I can never recall a winger giving him a roasting, and this was in an era when every team carried two wingers playing wide on the flanks. He could be tough to the point of brutal when necessary and many's the time he ended dangerous raids with perfectly timed tackles. He was steady and reliable, just what you want from a full back. It is not a position for Fancy Dans. Our supporters sometimes gave him a tough time for being caught out of position, but they lost sight of the fact that he was often covering for Danny, who was not the greatest defensive player in the world!"

RON HENRY

Born Shoreditch, August 17 1934. Played 247 League matches for Tottenham between 1954 and 1965 before becoming a highly regarded youth coach. He was at left-back in all 42 of Tottenham's League matches in the 1960-61 season. Early in his career with Redbourne he had been a skilful left winger, and then switched to wing-half and later, on turning professional with Tottenham, settled down at left back. He made his League debut at centre-half against Huddersfield in 1955, but it was not until the 1959-60 season that he took over the No 3 shirt from Welsh international Mel Hopkins. Capped once, in Sir Alf Ramsey's first match as the England manager against France in 1963. England were beaten 5-2 and Ron did not get another chance.

BILL NICK APPRAISAL: "I had the difficult decision of choosing between Ron and Welsh international Mel Hopkins at left back. In fact it was not until Mel was sidelined by a broken nose that Ron became the automatic choice, and in that Double season he proved he was well worthy of his place. He was an ever-present along with Blanchflower, White and Allen, and seemed to grow with every game. He was brilliant at making sliding tackles, looked composed on the ball, and was clever at jockeying wingers until they ran out of space. As with any player brought up to think the Spurs way Ron could play the ball out of defence with accuracy and in a positive manner. Like me, he won just one England cap. He deserved more."

DANNY BLANCHFLOWER

Born Belfast, February 10 1926. Played 337 League games for Tottenham between 1954 and 1963 after service with Glentoran, Barnsley and Aston Villa. One of the most creative and authoritative players ever to set foot on a football pitch, he was a born leader who, as well as skippering Spurs through their 'glory-glory' years, also captained the Northern Ireland team that reached the quarter-finals of the 1958 World Cup. His younger brother, Jack, was a prominent centre-half who never played again after surviving the Manchester United air crash at Munich in 1958. Danny was twice voted the Footballer of the Year before a recurring knee injury forced his retirement in 1963.

BILL NICK APPRAISAL: "Danny had a spell on the transfer list in my early days as coach, but I had no intention of letting him go. I knew how important he was to the club as a born leader on and off the pitch. He was a captain in every sense of the word, inspiring the players around him with his highly skilled football and lifting them with words of wisdom. His contribution went much farther and deeper than his performances on the playing field. He was a great reader of the game, and had an in-built radar system that guided him to the right places at the right times. His weakness was that he put so much thought into attacking play that he sometimes forgot his defensive responsibilities. We had words over that! He was a true master of the footballing arts. and an inspiring leader on and off the pitch."

MAURICE NORMAN

Born Mulbarton, Norfolk, May 8 1934. Played 357 League matches for Spurs between 1955 and 1965, following one full season with his local club, Norwich City. He was England's centre-half in 23 international matches and was shortlisted for World Cup duty in 1966 when his career was finished by a broken leg received in a Spurs friendly against the Hungarian national team in 1965. At 6ft 1in and 13 stone, he stood like an immovable mountain in the middle of the Spurs defence. He had joined Tottenham as a full-back, but it was his switch to centre-half in succession to Harry Clarke that established him as one of the most reliable defenders in the League.

BILL NICK APPRAISAL: "Maurice was a Jimmy Anderson signing, and became an exceptional defender. He was big in build, big in heart and big in personality. Strangely enough he was not that commanding in the air, but he was so tall that he usually got to the high balls before rival forwards had started jumping. He helped make goalkeeper Bill Brown's job easier with his expert covering and support play. On those occasions when the usually dependable Brown made a mess of a cross you would usually find Maurice thumping the ball away. Maurice would not claim to have been the most skilful centre-half, but he had immense strength and was reliable and a totally committed competitor. But for tragically breaking a leg I am sure he would have been England's centre-half in the 1966 World Cup finals and Jack Charlton might never have got his chance. That's football for you. Full of cruel and unexpected twists."

DAVE MACKAY

Born Edinburgh, Nov. 14 1934. Scored 42 goals in 268 League appearances for Tottenham after joining them from Hearts for £30,000 in March 1959. While with Hearts he won Scottish League Cup, Scottish Cup and Scottish League championship medals; then with Spurs he collected three FA Cup winners' medals, a League Championship medal and a European Cup Winners' Cup medal, although missing the final because of injury. Later, with Derby County, he won a Second Division Championship medal; and as manager he steered Derby to the First Division title in 1974-75. He also managed Swindon, Nottingham Forest and Walsall before coaching in the Middle East. He twice made come-backs after breaking a leg. He shared the Footballer of the Year award with Tony Book in 1969 and won 22 Scottish caps..

BILL NICK APPRAISAL: "I've often gone on record as saying that Dave Mackay was my best signing. I did not just get a player from Hearts, I got a motivator. He could bring the best out of his team-mates by his effort and enthusiasm, not only during matches but also on the training pitch. Dave gave 100 per cent every time he played and was the heart and soul of the team. He had an incredible will to win and this rubbed off on every player. While he was a powerful player with a shuddering tackle, he also had delicate skill and an educated left foot. It was remarkable the way he came back as a vital force after twice breaking a leg. He was a manager's dream."

TERRY DYSON

Born Malton, North Yorkshire, November 29 1934. Played 184 League games for Spurs and scored 41 goals. The son of famous jockey 'Ginger' Dyson, he came to White Hart Lane from non-League Scarborough in 1955. He was a member of the first-team squad until 1965 when he moved on to Fulham and then Colchester and Guildford City. A regular in the Double-winning side, he scored two goals that clinched victory in the European Cup Winners' Cup final in 1963. In 1961 he became the first Spurs player to score a hat-trick in the derby against Arsenal (Spurs won 4-3). He later became an assessor of schoolboy footballers for the Football Association.

BILL NICK APPRAISAL: "Terry Dyson was a determined competitor who never let the side down. His grit and whole-hearted endeavour just gave him the edge over the more composed Medwin, who was desperately unlucky with injuries. Terry D. would run his legs off for the team, and often popped up with vital winning goals. He, of course, had the most memorable match of his career in the Cup Winners' Cup final. He continually had the Atletico Madrid defence in trouble with his thrusting runs, and his two goals turned the match. He was big enough to admit he did not have the skill of some of those tremendous players around him, but he more than made up for it with his effort. Terry's enthusiasm was infectious and you could always count on him to run himself into the ground for the team."

JOHN WHITE

Born Musselburgh, Lothian, April 28 1937. Scored 40 goals in 183 League games for Spurs after joining them from Falkirk in 1959 for a bargain price £20,000. He was capped 22 times by Scotland and was an 'ever present' for Spurs during the Double season. In his youth he had been turned down by both Glasgow Rangers and Middlesbrough as being too small, but he quickly showed that his frail appearance was misleading when starting his career with Alloa Athletic and then Falkirk. Bill Nicholson bought him on the advice of both Dave Mackay and Danny Blanchflower, who had seen him in action for Scotland. The year after helping Spurs capture the Cup Winners' Cup in 1963 he was struck down and killed by a bolt of lightning while sheltering under a tree during a solo round of golf.

BILL NICK APPRAISAL: "I still get very emotional when I think of the cruel way John was taken from us. He was a great player when he died, and I am convinced he was going to get better. He was so aptly nicknamed 'The Ghost of White Hart Lane.' It was his ability off the ball that made him such a phenomenal player. He would pop up from out of nowhere just when he was needed most to make a pass or collect the ball. Like Danny Blanchflower, he had the gift of being able to give the exact weight to a pass. John was a former cross country runner who had the energy to run all day and could cut a defence in half with just one cunningly placed ball. With White, Blanchflower and Mackay operating together in midfield we just could not go wrong."

BOBBY SMITH

Born Lingdale, North Yorkshire, February 22 1933. Scored 176 goals in 271 League matches for Spurs after joining them from Chelsea in 1955. Wound down his League career with Brighton, his 18 goals in 31 matches helping them win the Fourth Division Championship in 1965. He scored 13 goals in 15 appearances as England centre-forward, all but one of them in partnership with Jimmy Greaves. In the Double season he was top First Division marksman for Spurs with 28 goals and he netted in each of the successive FA Cup final victories. He and Les Allen were lethal together in 1960-61, continuing a double act that had started at Stamford Bridge.

BILL NICK APPRAISAL: "Because he could be a battering-ram style of centre-forward, Bobby was rarely given the credit he deserved for his high level of skill. People seemed to think he was all brute force. Strength certainly played an important part in his game, and he used to make full use of his heavyweight physique. But he also had subtle touches and could lay off delicate passes. He was the perfect partner for Les Allen and then Jimmy and he assisted in many of their goals. He used to win the ball for Les and Jimmy in the air, removing a defender or two with the sheer force of his challenge. Foreign goalkeepers used to be petrified of him in the days when players were allowed to let them know they were around. He was magnificent in that Double season, and when he had to miss a few games because of injury young Frank Saul did an excellent stand-in job for us."

LES ALLEN

Born Dagenham, Essex, September 4 1937. Scored 47 goals in 119 League matches for Spurs. Started his career as an amateur with Briggs Sports while working as an apprentice with the local Ford factory. Signed for Chelsea in 1954 and netted 11 goals in 44 League appearances before joining Tottenham in December 1959. Making way for the arrival of Jimmy Greaves, he joined Queen's Park Rangers and helped them become the first Third Division side to win the League Cup at Wembley. He scored 55 goals in 128  League games for QPR before starting a management career during which he was in charge at Loftus Road and at Swindon, and then in Salonika, Greece. He later became a skilled model maker, and in retirement shared his time between his homes in Essex and Cyprus. From a famous football family, his brother Dennis, sons Clive and Bradley, and nephews Martin and Paul all made an impact as professionals.

BILL NICK APPRAISAL: "A much-underrated player, Les had a prolific partnership with Bobby Smith, and together they played a major part in clinching the League and Cup double. Les was a neat, constructive centre-forward or inside-forward with a fine turn of speed, an accurate right foot shot, and excellent positional sense. He was unlucky not to get international recognition. I got him in a swap deal for Johnny Brooks when Les was languishing in Chelsea reserves, and I definitely got the better of the deal. He did a superb job for us and I felt sorry for him when he lost his place to Greavsie. But these things happen in football. Nobody's place is guaranteed."

CLIFF JONES

Born Swansea February 7 1935. Scored 135 goals in 318 League matches for Spurs after joining them from Swansea for £35,000 in February 1958. He won 59 Welsh international caps and had the final shots of his career with Fulham, for whom he signed in 1968 after collecting a string of honours with Spurs. He stood 5ft 7in tall, weighed just over 10 stone, and moved like a whippet along either wing for Spurs and Wales. He was the son of pre-war Welsh international Ivor Jones, and the nephew of former Arsenal and Wales inside-forward Bryn, and the brother of long-serving League professional Bryn Jnr. His cousin, Ken Jones, was an ex-professional who became one of the country's leading sports columnists.

BILL NICK APPRAISAL: "The remarkable thing about Cliff was that he was a right footed player, yet had his best moments on the left wing. At his peak, he was without question one of the world's greatest wingers. When he was in full flight I doubt if there was a more dangerous forward on the ball. He used to run with the pace, determination and bravery of a Welsh wing three-quarter. He was brave to the point of madness in the penalty area. It was a common sight to see Cliff rising like a salmon at the far post to head spectacular goals that were amazing when you realise he was a smallish bloke with a slim frame. When you talk about great wingers like Matthews, Finney and Best you can mention Jonesie in the same breath. He was as effective as any of them, and on either wing."

These, then, were the players who collectively achieved the greatest season in Tottenham's history. Yet at the end of it ultra perfectionist Bill Nicholson was dissatisfied. "We just did not perform in the final against Leicester." he groaned for years afterwards. "I wanted us to win in true Spurs style. Our victory left me feeling flat and frustrated."

The warm human side that Bill usually managed to hide from the public and the media came out after the final when he filled the FA Cup with champagne and took it into the Leicester City dressing-room, where their exhausted players were still in the bath. He made sure the Cup was passed to every one of them and said: "You can feel proud of your performance today. To be down to virtually ten men and battle like you did was exceptional. Well done."

My old mate Frank McLintock, a four-times Wembley loser who later got his well-deserved glory with Arsenal, told me: "That was typical Bill. I can't think of another manager who would have thought of the opponents in a moment like that. We did not feel disgraced and knew we had given a good account of ourselves against one of the greatest club teams of all time. To have Bill Nicholson confirming how well we had played was a very special moment. He was a manager I would loved to have played for. A true master."

Even the after-match banquet at the Savoy Hotel fell flat. The star of the cabaret, Shirley Bassey, pulled out at the last minute because of a throat infection.

"It just shows how plans can go wrong on and off the pitch," said a glum Bill Nick. He had the League Championship trophy and the FA Cup, the first manager of the century to achieve the "impossible" double. The one thing he did not have was complete satisfaction.

But there were a lot of golden moments still to come to cheer Bill up and satisfy even his high standards.

They kicked off with the arrival of a player who cost one pound under £100,000. Enter Greavsie.

Chapter Five
The Greavsie
Factor

BILL NICHOLSON did not want to burden Jimmy with being the first £100,000 footballer, and so he negotiated a £99,999 fee to bring him home from Italy, where he had spent a miserable five months after joining them from Chelsea in May 1961.

It was the start of a mutual love affair between Greavsie and the Tottenham fans as he set about building a mountain of goals that lifted him into a lasting place in White Hart Lane legend.

The 1960s were about much more than just England's long-awaited triumph in the World Cup. The decade heralded the first success in Europe of British clubs led by Tottenham; saw the long overdue introduction of substitutes, ushered in the ee-aye-adio revolution on Merseyside; and witnessed the kicking out of the maximum wage to lead the way to today's professional footballers swimming in money. The sixties were all about the Beatles, rock 'n' roll, Mini-cars, mini-skirts, sarcasm-masquerading-as-satire, Clay-AKA-Ali and, of course, George Best.

It was a swinging time for everybody apart from those footballers who found themselves redundant as clubs made swingeing cuts to help pay their suddenly inflated wage bills. Spurs prudently paid each of their first-team players £65 a week, with Bill Nick earning just £50. His players always earned more than he did.

Fulham's bearded wonder Jimmy Hill led the PFA's campaign to kick out the £20 maximum wage as the eloquent union chairman, and it was his Craven Cottage team-mate Johnny Haynes who made the quickest profit. Comedian Tommy Trinder, chairman of Fulham, announced to the press in 1961 that he was making England skipper Haynes British football's first £100-a-week footballer. "It was," admitted Johnny, "the funniest thing Tommy ever said."

The players owed a big vote of thanks and a few bottles of bubbly to England inside-forward George Eastham, who stood alone against the football barons. He battled in the High Court against what was described as "a slave contract" and the restraint of trade. Eastham started his one-man war while at Newcastle and finally won it after moving to Arsenal in November 1960. He was the Bosman of his time, and does not get enough credit for his courage in taking on, and beating, the establishment.

The Football League caved in after the players once again threatened strike action, and this time they really did mean it. In the space of a week in January 1961 the maximum wage was kicked out and the restrictive contracts scrapped. Suddenly the likes of Greavsie, Denis Law, Joe Baker and Gerry Hitchens found they could earn in England the same sort of money that had tempted them to be lured by the lira to Italy.

Here's Greavsie talking about those early days as a Spurs player, Bill Nick and his move from Milan to Tottenham in that historic £99,999 deal:

•I considered myself the luckiest footballer on earth the day Bill Nick arrived in Milan to sign me for Tottenham. Not only was he rescuing me from what I reckoned was the prison of Italian football, but he was also giving me the chance to join what I believed was the finest club side in Europe. It was in the previous season that Spurs had pulled off that historic Double. I had played against them with Chelsea, and I can vouch for the fact that they were, to use a Cockney understatement, 'a bit tasty.'

They purred along like a Rolls Royce, with Danny Blanchflower, John White and Dave Mackay at the wheel. When they wanted to touch the accelerator there was Cliff Jones to break the speed limit down either wing; and if they needed a full show of horsepower, Bobby Smith was put in the driving seat. These were the nucleus of five world-class players around which Bill Nick had built his team. He had got the perfect blend and I remember thinking when I played against them, 'Blimey, there's not a weakness in this team. They can win the lot.'

'The lot' in those days meant the League Championship and FA Cup, two trophies that were harder to win then because – and of this I am convinced – the game was a lot tougher and more demanding. In comparison, today's football has become a virtual non-contact sport. And remember we were all on a twenty quid a week maximum wage at the time, which is why I nipped off to Italy.

Just to give you an idea of the overall standard of the First Division in 1960-61: I was playing in a Chelsea side that included such international-class players as Peter Bonetti, Frank Blunstone, Peter Brabrook, Bobby Evans, Bobby Tambling and Terry Venables. I managed to bang in 41 goals that season. We finished in twelfth place in the table.

Wolves, dripping with international players, scored 103 First Division goals and could do no better than third. Defending champions Burnley, blessed with the talents of Jimmy McIlroy, Jimmy Anderson, Alex Elder, Jimmy Robson, Ray Pointer, John Connelly, Brian Miller and Gordon Harris, netted 102 First Division goals, and were back in fourth place. We were all puffing and panting trying to keep up with Spurs.

Runners-up Sheffield Wednesday had England inter-nationals Tony Kay, Peter Swan, Ron Springett and John Fantham at their peak. Blackpool missed relegation by a point, despite being able to call on such skilled players as Tony Waiters, Jimmy Armfield, Ray Parry, Ray Charnley and the one and only Stanley Matthews. Each team also had at least two hatchet men, with instructions to stop the clever players playing.

The like of 'Bites Yer Legs' Norman Hunter, Tommy Smith and Chopper Harris were coming through the

SCRAPBOOK MEMORIES: Greavsie and Terry Venables were a couple of Cockney conmen against Liverpool at the Lane in 1968. Tel prepared to take a free-kick and then went down on one knee to tie up a boot lace that didn't need tying. The Liverpool wall relaxed and Jimmy sent a banana-style free-kick swinging into their net. Bend it like Greavsie!

ranks and about to make themselves felt. Just talking about them brings me out in bruises. In today's game they would have been red carded every time they stepped on a pitch if they tried to tackle as they did in those 1960s when football was not for the faint-hearted.

There was class running right the way through the First Division – and not a foreign player in sight. This was the quality of the opposition that Bill Nicholson's 'Super Spurs' side had to overcome to pull off the League and Cup Double that had eluded every great team throughout the 20th Century. They did it with a style and flair that made them one of the most attractive teams of all time. There were defensive deficiencies, but you never heard a murmur of complaint from the spectators, who were always given tremendous value for money.

For me to join the team in 1961 was like being given a passport to paradise. I considered it like coming home. I was a Spurs fan when I was a kid, and it was odds-on my joining them from school until a lovely rascal of a Chelsea scout called Jimmy Thompson sweet-talked my Dad into encouraging me to go to Stamford Bridge.

I wondered how the Tottenham fans would react to me moving to their manor at White Hart Lane, and realized they were quite keen on the idea when I played my first game in a Spurs shirt in a reserve match at Plymouth.

There was a record crowd for a reserve game of 13,000 at Home Park and I know many of them were Spurs supporters, because over the years I have met loads that say they were there!

My other concern was how the Spurs players would take to me. They had been reading the day-to-day accounts of my exploits in Italy, where I had been waging a verbal war in a bid to get back into British football. Those who knew me only by reputation must have been thinking I was a real troublemaker, and – having just won the 'impossible' Double without me – understandably looked on me as an intruder who could possibly rock their happy and successful boat.

Thank goodness it didn't take me long to kick their doubts into touch. I got lucky and kicked off with a hat-trick against Blackpool in my first-team debut, and I settled into the side – both on and off the pitch – as if I had been at Tottenham all my life.

I am never comfortable talking about goals that I scored, but I have to admit that one of the goals in my first match was a little bit special. Dave Mackay took one of his long throw-ins, Terry Medwin flicked the ball on, and I scored with what the newspapers described as 'a spectacular scissors kick.' From that moment on I was accepted by the Tottenham fans and players as 'one of them'.

All these years later I can say that the Tottenham team of that period was the best side I ever played with, and that takes into account England matches.

Good old reliable Bill Nick kept his word on everything he told me when persuading me to join Spurs when the easy option would have been to go back to Chelsea, who were also trying to buy me from Milan. '

Tottenham made a monumental bid for the major prize – the European Cup – in Jimmy's first season, during which the 'Glory-Glory-hallelujah' choruses raised the White Hart Lane roof. There are conflicting opinions as to when the 'Battle Hymn of the Republic' was adopted as the club's theme song. Some insist it was being sung by Spurs supporters at Molineux in April 1960 as Tottenham powered to a 3-1 victory that stopped Wolves being first to the League and Cup Double.

Older supporters vaguely remember it being sung back in the early 1950s after a cartoon had appeared in the Tottenham match programme showing Arthur Rowe day dreaming of the Double. The caption read: "While the Spurs go marching on ..."

There was an explosion of noise every time Spurs played

European Cup ties at White Hart Lane in 1961-62 as they saw off Gornik, Feyenoord and Dukla Prague. There was also good humour to go with the fanatical support. A small group of Spurs supporters always dressed as angels, carrying witty placards and waving them – without malice – at opposition fans. There was never a hint of hooliganism. That scar on the face of soccer was a decade away. And not a mention of the 'Y' word.

Tottenham were desperately unlucky to lose a two-leg European Cup semi-final against eventual champions Benfica, propelled by the rising master Eusebio. To this day, Greavsie insists that a 'goal' he scored, which would have put Spurs into the final, was wrongly flagged offside.

Bill Nick quickly picked them up after their exit from Europe and the following month they retained the FA Cup, with Jimmy Greaves scoring an exquisite goal in the third minute to put them on the way to an impressive 3-1 victory over Burnley.

My Greavsie bias coming out again, but I think it rates with the finest goals scored at old Wembley. He was fifteen yards out and *passed* the ball along the ground into the net through a forest of players' legs and with all the unerring accuracy of a Jack Nicklaus putt. Jimmy, never one to boast in his playing days, said just before the players left the dressing-room, "I'm going to get an early one today lads." If it had been a fluke it would have been an outstanding goal, so the fact that Greavsie meant it puts it up into the classic category.

The Tottenham team:

Brown; Baker, Henry; Blanchflower, Norman, Mackay; Medwin, White, Smith, Greaves, Jones.

Goals from Bobby Smith and skipper Danny Blanchflower clinched Tottenham's win after Jimmy Robson had equalized for Burnley. Danny's goal came from the penalty spot in the 80th minute after Tommy Cummings had handled a Terry Medwin shot on the goal-line.

As Blanchflower was placing the ball on the penalty spot his

Northern Ireland team-mate and good friend Jimmy McIlroy said to him: "Bet you miss."

Danny did not say a word. He calmly sent goalkeeper Adam Blacklaw the wrong way as he stroked the penalty home. As he ran past Burnley schemer McIlory, he said: "Bet I don't!"

The victory earned Tottenham a place in the European Cup Winners' Cup, and the 'Glory-Glory' chanting supporters roared them all the way into the final in May 1963. No British team had won a major trophy in Europe when Spurs travelled to Rotterdam for the final, and hopes that they could break the duck were suddenly diminished when their main motivator, Dave Mackay, failed a fitness test on the day of the match.

The absence of Mackay was a devastating blow because he had been a major force in Tottenham's magnificent success over the previous two seasons. As it sank in that they would have to perform without his battering ram backing a blanket of gloom dropped on the Spurs camp.

Atletico were suddenly considered by neutrals to be warm favourites to retain the trophy they had won in impressive style the previous year, when they mastered a high-quality Fiorentina side.

Mackay's absence plunged Bill Nick into a morose mood, and he added to the air of pessimism when he ran through the strengths of the opposition during a tactical team talk. He made Atletico sound like the greatest team ever to run on to a football pitch, and he bruised rather than boosted the confidence of his players.

Skipper Blanchflower was so concerned about the sudden gloom and doom environment that he summoned all the players to a private meeting and made one of the most inspiring speeches of his career.

Using a mixture of fact and blarney, word-master Blanchflower pumped confidence back into his team-mates and made them believe in their ability to win. He countered every point that Bill Nicholson had made about the Madrid players by underlining

Jimmy Greavses, the artist captured by an artist

Tottenham's strengths, and he convinced them that they were superior to the Spaniards in every department. It was a speech of Churchillian class and Tottenham went into the final with renewed determination to take the trophy back to White Hart Lane.

This was how Tottenham lined up for the game of their lives, with Tony Marchi stepping into Dave Mackay's place:

Brown, Baker, Henry, Blanchflower, Norman, Marchi, Jones, White, Smith, Greaves, Dyson

Bill Nick, one of the finest tacticians in the game, deserved the credit for the fact that Greavsie was in position to give Spurs the lead in the 16th minute. He had spotted, during a spying mission to Madrid, that the Atletico defence was slow to cover down the left side, and he instructed that full use should be made of the blistering speed of Cliff Jones. Moving with pace and penetration, Cliff sprinted to meet a neatly placed pass from Bobby Smith and Greavsie drifted into the middle to steer his accurate centre into the net with his deadly left foot. It was a real pick-pocket job, and Tottenham's fans roared their 'Glory-Glory' anthem as the Spaniards suddenly wilted.

It was on the wings that Tottenham were monopolizing the match, with Jones and tiny Terry Dyson running the Spanish full-backs into dizzy disorder. Atletico, strangely enough, also had a winger called Jones, but he was not in the same class as Tottenham's Welsh wizard.

The on-fire Dyson and Jones who combined to set up goal number two in the 32nd minute, exchanging passes before releasing the ball to Smith, who laid it back for John White to rifle a low shot into the net.

This was a rare but crucial goal for White, who had made his reputation as a maker rather than taker of goals. His signature was stamped on most of Tottenham's attacks as he prised open the Atletico defence with beautifully weighted passes. Blanchflower,

White and the tall, stately Marchi were working like Trojans in midfield to make up for the absence of the one and only Mackay. At most clubs, Marchi would have been an automatic choice for the first team, and he played with such skill and determination that his contribution was in the Mackay class. There can be no higher praise.

Atletico Madrid revived their flickering flame of hope in the first minute of the second-half when Collar scored from the penalty spot after Ron Henry had fisted the ball off the goal-line.

For 20 minutes there was a danger that Spurs could lose their way as the Cup-holders forced a series of corner-kicks, but the defence managed to survive the Spanish storm.

Goalkeeper Bill Brown took his life in his hands as he threw himself courageously at the feet of Mendonca to snatch the ball off the forward's toes. Chuzo broke free and Tottenham's fans sighed with relief as he shot the wrong side of the post; then Ramiro drove the ball just off target. This was when everybody connected with Tottenham began to wonder and worry whether they were going to get by without the great Mackay, who in a situation like this would have been breaking Spanish hearts with his thundering tackles and brandishing a fist in a demand for extra effort from all his team-mates.

It was 'Dynamo' Dyson, having the game of a lifetime, who ended the Atletico comeback when his hanging cross was fumbled into the net by goalkeeper Madinabeytia, who had one eye on the menacing presence of beefy Bobby Smith.

Dyson became a man inspired and laid on a second goal for Greavsie before putting the seal on a memorable performance with a scorching shot at the end of a weaving 30-yard run. His first goal was something of a fluke, but the second was a masterpiece.

As Tottenham's triumphant players paraded the Cup in front of their ecstatic fans, Bobby Smith shouted at Dyson in his typically blunt way: "If I were you, mate, I'd hang up my boots. There's no way you can top that. You were out of this world."

The following season dawned with no hint that it was to see the

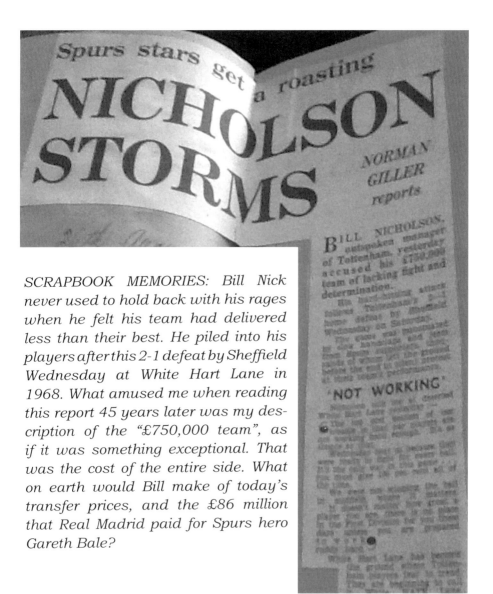

SCRAPBOOK MEMORIES: Bill Nick never used to hold back with his rages when he felt his team had delivered less than their best. He piled into his players after this 2-1 defeat by Sheffield Wednesday at White Hart Lane in 1968. What amused me when reading this report 45 years later was my description of the "£750,000 team", as if it was something exceptional. That was the cost of the entire side. What on earth would Bill make of today's transfer prices, and the £86 million that Real Madrid paid for Spurs hero Gareth Bale?

break-up of The Team That Bill Built. The heart was ripped out of 'Super Spurs' in a tragic and painful way, and a black cloud of despondency enveloped the club.

The nightmare was slow and drawn out. It started on the evening of December 10 1963 at Old Trafford, when Tottenham were playing Manchester United in the second-leg of a European Cup Winners' Cup tie. Dave Mackay broke a leg in a collision with Noel Cantwell that surely left the United skipper losing sleep about the validity of his challenge.

Just a few weeks later, Danny Blanchflower was forced to retire because of a recurring knee injury. Tottenham had lost the brains of the team and the heart of the team, and worse was to follow at the end of the season. John White, the eyes of the team, was sitting under a tree sheltering from a storm on a North London golf course when he was tragically killed by lightning. Tottenham had lost the three most vital cogs in their machine.

Bill Nicholson had to handle his grief over the loss of John White while getting busy in the transfer market. He bought Alan Mullery from Fulham, Laurie Brown from Arsenal, Cyril Knowles from Middlesbrough, Pat Jennings from Watford, Jimmy Robertson from St Mirren and Alan Gilzean from Dundee.

He took a breather, and then went shopping again, this time buying centre-half Mike England from Blackburn and Terry Venables from Chelsea.

It was like putting together a huge jigsaw, with the success-hungry fans showing little patience as Bill tried to get the pieces to fit. Terry Venables and Alan Mullery, in particular, were given a rough ride by supporters expecting them to produce the Blanchflower/White magic overnight

Because Bill was often as expressionless as a sphinx, people looking in from the outside thought he was taking all the changes in his stride. Only those close to him realised the toll it was taking.

It was some years later when Bill revealed to me the enormous stress he'd been under in those months when his great 'Super Spurs' side started to fall apart:

•The worst blow, of course, was losing John White in such tragic circumstances, and it was not that long after we had mourned the loss to cancer of his father-in-law Harry Evans, who was doing a wonderful job as my assistant.

John's death was just about the worst news I've ever had. When the police phoned to tell me John had been killed by lightning I thought it was a hoax, because twice in the previous week idiots had phoned me to say Greavsie had been killed in a car crash. I at first told the caller he was sick, but when it dawned on me that it was the truth I was distraught.

I had to identify John at the mortuary, the hardest thing I ever had to do. Cecil Poynton came with me, and we both left in tears. To see John lying there looking as if he had just fallen off to sleep was heart breaking. Such a waste.

I often think the club could have done a lot more to look after John's wife and family. I wish I'd had the time to give the matter more attention, but I was up to my neck in trying to get the club back on an even keel.

It was easily the toughest challenge of my managerial career, rebuilding the team, but it was even tougher for the players and in particular Mullery and Venables. They were having to fill the gaps left by two Tottenham idols, Danny Blanchflower and John White. I don't like the use of the word legends, but Danny and John certainly came into that category.

We had spoiled the Spurs supporters with our success, and they had little patience waiting for Alan and Terry to fit in. Putting a new team together co-incided with changes in the game. Teams were blindly copying Alf's 1966 England tactics and switching to 4-3-3 and then 4-4-2 and the football suddenly became tight and defensive, and there were ugly moods on the terraces because of the rise of hooliganism. They were not the best of times.•

Not the best of times, but Bill brightened them by creating another Cup-winning team. Here comes the spirit of '67.

Chapter Five
When Spurs
Got the Savoy Blues

BILL NICK was trying to build another 'Super Spurs'. He never quite made it. The new Tottenham team had some memorable moments together in the mid-sixties, but – let's be honest – they never touched the peak performances of the Blanchflower-White-Mackay era. How many times can you touch the Moon?

It was rumoured that Nicholson had tried to bring Edmonton-born England skipper Johnny Haynes to White Hart Lane to team up with his old England side-kick Jimmy Greaves. But Bill insisted this was media talk, and the Blanchflower-White roles went to Mullery and Venables. Good as they were, they were never able to match the impressive impact of Blanchflower and White.

Greavsie had become accustomed to the pace set by Danny and John, and he struggled to adapt to their style of delivery. Both were given a tough time by the Spurs supporters, who had been spoiled rotten over recent years. They unkindly but understandably compared the newcomers with their great idols.

Venables was not always happy playing at White Hart Lane after his success as the midfield boss at Chelsea, and when he eventually moved on to Queen's Park Rangers who would have taken any bets that one day he would return and buy a huge share in the club! Yes, as Greavsie says, it's a funny old game.

One of the new-look Tottenham squad who did win the hearts of the fans was Alan Gilzean, who formed a wonderful partnership with Greavsie. Jimmy found Gilly a joy to play with, and he felt that Alan was never given sufficient credit for his delicate touch play and finishing finesse in the penalty area. He was a master of the flick header, and could bamboozle defences with deceptive changes of pace and clever ball control.

Missing the command of Blanchflower, and the drive of Mackay, the 1963-64 season was relatively barren for Spurs after three years of non-stop success. But they still managed to finish fourth in the League Championship in a season that would be remembered for the start of Liverpool's 'Red Revolution' under the mesmeric management of Bill Shankly.

Ownership of the Spurs had moved from the Bearman family to the Wales late in 1960, with first Fred Wale and then Sidney as chairman. They considered Tottenham a family club, and allowed Bill Nick to get on with the job of managing without interference. Under the Wale influence, the Tottenham directors ran a tight, well-organised ship. Perhaps too tight, because in my opinion they never ever paid Bill the salary he deserved. But Bill being Bill he never complained and got on with his job. He was not doing it for the money. Bill refused to confirm it, but I got it on good authority that he never ever earned more than £200 a week as manager; and most of the time less than half that.

His latest team saved their peak performances for the FA Cup in the 1966-67 season, culminating in a well-earned FA Cup final triumph over London neighbours Chelsea at Wembley. Of the side that won the trophy in 1962, only Dave Mackay and Greavsie had survived, along with Cliff Jones on the substitute's bench. Greavsie had recovered from the hepatitis that had robbed him of half a yard of pace during the build-up to the 1966 World Cup finals; nobody ever takes that illness into account when discussing Jimmy's contribution to the World Cup triumph, halted by a shin injury received in a group game against France.

The fact that Mackay was there at the 1967 FA Cup final to lead out the Tottenham team as skipper was the sort of story that you would expect to come from the pages of Roy of the Rovers. 'Miracle Man' Mackay had made an astonishing recovery after breaking his leg a second time following his controversial collision with Noel Cantwell at Old Trafford in 1963.

Mackay motivated a team that had Pat Jennings building himself into a legend as the last line of defence. Baby-faced Irish

SCRAPBOOK MEMORIES: In all my years interviewing sportsmen, I never came across anybody to match the determination and desire that used to spill out of Dave Mackay. He made this 'I'm set to go back to Wembley' forecast two months before collecting the FA Cup in 1967 and after twice breaking a leg. He stood only just over 5ft 7in but always came across as a giant.

Mackay . . . will defiant

Mackay vows 'I'm set to go back to Wembley'

By NORMAN GILLER

DAVE MACKAY

dreams of leading Tottenham to the third F.A. Cup final of his career of courage.

Mackay the bold fired Spurs to the League-Cup double in 1961, the Cup in 1962, and the European Cup-winners' Cup in 1963.

Then he braved the agony

of a twice-broken left leg and nearly two years out of League soccer.

Now he is ready, defiant, still dominant, to spark Spurs to new triumphs.

"Listen to Mackay talking to me last night about the Cup.

"Wembley means everything to me. The one thing that really counts in a foot-

international Joe Kinnear had come in as right-back in place of the energetic Phil Beal, who was unlucky to break an arm after playing an important part in getting Spurs to the final. Joe, a neat, controlled player, was partnered at full-back by Cyril Knowles, a former Yorkshire miner who took the eye with his sharp tackling and some polished, if at times eccentric skills. He was to become a cult hero, with anything he attempted – good or bad – accompanied by choruses of 'Nice one, Cyril' from the White Hart Lane faithful. It was a chant that was to earn Cyril some nice bread from a television commercial.

Standing like a Welsh mountain in the middle of the defence was the majestic Mike England, one of the finest centre-halves ever produced in Britain. He was a class player from head to toe.

Dave Mackay was the immovable link between defence and attack as he adapted his game from buccaneer to anchorman, helping to stoke the fires of the engine room where Alan Mullery and Terry Venables were forging a productive partnership. They never quite approached the peaks that Spurs fans had seen in the 'Glory-Glory' days of Blanchflower-White-Mackay, but few midfield combinations have ever reached that sky-scraping standard.

Venables, with Cockney swagger and supreme confidence, had been the king of the castle at Stamford Bridge, to the point where Tommy Docherty was forced to say: "There's only one manager at Chelsea, and it isn't Terry Venables."

When he moved to the Lane Venners was quickly put in his place by Spurs tribal leader, Mackay the Braveheart, and they grew to respect each other after a brief and bloody fight in the Tottenham gym. Terry wore a ring that gashed Dave's face.

I tried to break the story at the time, but Bill Nicholson swore everybody to silence. "A minor skirmish that you often get in fully committed training games," was how he dismissed it." The team spirit was considerably strengthened by the run to Wembley.

Jimmy Robertson was a flying Scot on the right wing, where his speed was a vital asset for the G-men – Gilzean and Greaves, who had a telepathic understanding for where to be to get the best out of each other. For the final, Bill Nick preferred Frank Saul to the veteran Cliff Jones for the No 11 shirt. Frank, who had been a fringe player in the Double-winning squad, was more of a central striker than a winger, but he was a direct player with a good nose for goal. Cliff, and Joe Kirkup for Chelsea, were the first players to wear No 12 shirts in an FA Cup final. The Tottenham team:

Jennings, Kinnear, Knowles, Mullery, England, Mackay, Robertson, Greaves, Gilzean, Venables, Saul. Sub: Jones

Facing Tottenham in the first all-London final were Tommy Docherty's elegant but unpredictable Chelsea team. They had gone through an even more drastic rebuilding programme than Spurs, and Terry Venables was part of the upheaval when he moved on to Tottenham to make room the previous year for the arrival of Scotland's 'Wizard of Dribble', Charlie Cooke.

Peter 'Catty' Bonetti was their goalkeeper, as good a catcher of the ball as there was in world football. Allan Harris, preferred at right-back to usual choice Joe Kirkup, was a solid defender and a good balance for the marvellously skilled Eddie McCreadie, who had the ball control of a winger to go with his scything tackles.

Marvin 'Lou' Hinton was a sound centre-half with a good footballing brain, and making the earth tremble alongside him was poker-faced Ron 'Chopper' Harris, Allan's brother and one of the most feared ball-winners in the game. Young, always-cheerful John Hollins was a bundle of atomic energy at right-half, and aggressive Scot John Boyle played a utility role in midfield while wearing the No 11 shirt.

Filling the scheming role for Chelsea that had belonged to Venables was the dance master Cooke, a charismatic character known to his friends as 'Bonny Prince Charlie'. All the people who tried to compare Charlie with his predecessor Venables were wasting their breath. They were as alike as grass and granite. Charlie liked to hang on to the ball and run with it as if it was tied to his boot laces, while Terry let the ball do the work with precise passes that could have come out of the Push and Run coaching manual.

Chelsea relied on three main marksmen to get the ball into the net. Bobby Tambling, a faithful Stamford Bridge servant who had recently overtaken Greavsie's club goalscoring record, had a terrific turn of speed and was a deadly finisher. Tommy Baldwin, who had joined Chelsea in a part-exchange deal that took George 'Stroller' Graham to Arsenal eight months earlier, was nicknamed 'Sponge' because of the way he soaked up work (and off the park, beer!).

Then there was Tony Hateley, a master of the airways whom Tommy Docherty had bought from Aston Villa for £100,000 after his silkily skilled centre-forward Peter Osgood had broken a leg. While weak on the ground, Tony was a powerhouse header of the ball who learned a lot from the old head master Tommy Lawton while at Notts County. One day he would pass on all he knew to his son, Mark Hateley.

Masterminding the Chelsea team was manager Tommy Docherty, one of the game's great personalities. He had a razor-sharp Glaswegian wit and was in complete contrast to the often cautious and tight-lipped Bill Nicholson.

I brought The Doc and Nick together for a question and answer session for the *Daily Express* during the build-up to the Final. It was my reward for helping the Anglo-American Sporting Club set up a dinner honouring the two teams at the Park Lane Hilton on the Tuesday before their showdown. I had been instrumental in helping to form the AASC four years earlier in a PR capacity for boxing entrepreneurs Jarvis Astaire and Mickey Duff, who organised a £5,000 payment into each of the players' pools in return for both squads dining with the members, many of whom were the wealthiest Tottenham and Chelsea supporters.

With the FA Cup on a table beside us, I was given ten minutes to ask the Doc and Bill Nick just five questions. Both were in dinner jackets, which gave a sophisticated edge to the interview.

SCRAPBOOK MEMORIES: Tommy Doc and Bill Nick with the FA Cup on the Tuesday before the 1967 Final. Bill rubbed it with a handkerchief, getting it polished for the Spurs cabinet.

Tommy seized on the head-to-head session to try to score points, which pushed Bill into being less than his usual guarded and considered self:

"This is the first all-London final in the 98-year history of the FA Cup. What does it mean to the two clubs?"

The Doc: It gives the game an extra edge, and if – when – we win the Cup it will provide massive bragging rights for our supporters. There's always been huge rivalry between the two clubs and this is the opportunity for us to show we have overtaken Spurs as the No 1 club in the capital.

Bill Nick: You're jumping the gun there a bit, Tom. We're equally confident we can win, and have the proudest of all pedigrees at Wembley. Chelsea have never played there.

The Doc: That's yesterday's news, Bill, when you had one of the finest club teams I've ever seen and I bow to you for what you achieved in the Double year. But that's in the past and, with the greatest respect, your present Tottenham team is not in the same class as the 60-61 team – thank goodness.

Bill Nick: But you haven't seen the best of this side. I'm confident that you will on Saturday.

"All eyes are going to be on the midfield duel between Terry Venables and the man who replaced him at Chelsea, Charlie Cooke. How do they compare?"

The Doc: They're alike as chalk and cheese. Terry likes the ball to do the work, while Charlie can run any defence into the ground. I know which player I would least like to mark. Charlie can thread a ball through the eye of a needle, and then make it sit up and talk.

Bill Nick: It's all very well running with the ball and dribbling, but it's what you are allowed to do with it at the time of release that matters. I would much rather have Terry's passing accuracy, and he never delays our attacks by holding on too long.

The Doc: We'll see how Terry fancies concentrating on his passing when he sees Ron Harris advancing on him.

Bill Nick: So Harris is going to mark Venables, not Greaves?

The Doc: You're not going to trick me into revealing our tactics, Bill. Terry and Jimmy will both struggle to sleep on Friday night when they think about Chopper.

Bill Nick: I think your players might have a certain Dave Mackay on their minds. He has performed miracles to get back into shape and is tackling as hard as ever.

The Doc: It's great to see Dave back, a true hero. But he's in for a disappointment on Saturday. Our name's on the Cup.

Bill Nick: Nobody's name is on the Cup until the engraver knows the winners. I think it fair to call it an evenly balanced match, but I'm confident we will be taking the Cup home with us.

"Spurs have another Chelsea 'old boy' in Jimmy Greaves. He always scores in the important games."

The Doc (chuckling): Not in the World Cup final, he didn't. I thought Alf was mad to leave him out, and I don't think Jimmy's been the same player since. That decision to leave him out of the final must have knocked the stuffing out of him.

Bill Nick: It was the attack of hepatitis in the autumn of 1965 that took the edge off Jimmy's game, but he has shown this season he's shaken it off and got his old appetite back. He's scored twenty-nine League and Cup goals so far this season, and he and Gilzean have been outstanding on the way to Wembley.

"Chelsea have been having success with the experiment of playing Marvin Hinton as a sweeper. Can we expect to see that system on Saturday?"

The Doc: No, we're putting it on the back burner until next season. I'm not kicking it out forever, but I think we will be tighter and more disciplined with a conventional defensive line-up in the final. Marvin will play his usual centre-half role with which he is familiar and feels comfortable.

Bill Nick: I'm not sure we should be talking tactics to each other. Change the subject (Bill told me later that he was secretly delighted to hear Tommy was dropping the sweeper system and he thought it increased Tottenham's victory chances. He added that he could not believe that the Doc had revealed such an important tactical decision to his rival manager!).

"Spurs failed to beat Chelsea in the two First Division matches, 1-1 at the Lane and 3-0 to Chelsea at the Bridge. Does that give Chelsea a psychological advantage?"

The Doc: We deserved all four points, and the Spurs players know it. We have proved we're the better team twice already this season. It should have been 3-1 at the Lane, and our 3-0 victory at the Bridge flattered Tottenham. We will be looking to repeat it at Wembley on Saturday."

Bill Nick: Tom, have a look at the League table. We finished third, Chelsea ninth. That tells the true story of the form of the clubs going into the Final. The advantage is definitely with us.

I judged our short debate a draw, and it whetted the appetite for a match that, on paper, looked certain to be a cracker. But on the pitch it turned out to be something of a damp squib. The whole day fell a bit flat, mainly due to the fact that both teams were from London. That robbed the match of much of its atmosphere, because the supporters were not in that bubbling 'Oop f'the Coop' day-out mood.

Spurs skipper Mackay had a personal mission to win after having been inactive for so long, and he drove the Tottenham team on like a man possessed. They were always playing the more positive and purposeful football, and deserved their lead just before half-time. Jimmy Robertson crashed a shot wide of Bonetti after Alan Mullery's long-range pile-driver had been blocked.

SCRAPBOOK MEMORIES: George Graham got married in the morning with Terry Venables as his best man. In the afternoon they played against each other in the 1967 North London Derby at Highbury. George was the best man in a 4-0 Arsenal victory. Who would have thought that two decades later they would be taking turns on the Tottenham managerial roundabout.

Robertson, proving one of the most effective of all the forwards, set up a second goal in the sixty-eighth minute when he steered a typical long throw-in from Dave Mackay into the path of Frank Saul, who pivoted and hooked the ball high into the net.

Tottenham then slowed the game down to suit themselves, playing possession football so that Charlie Cooke could not get the ball to take command with his mesmerizing control. Bobby Tambling was allowed in for a goal five minutes from the end, but Tottenham tightened up at the back to hold out for a well-earned victory.

Bill Nick, a master of understatement, said:

All in all a satisfactory season. We finished third in the League just four points behind champions Manchester United and won the FA Cup for a third time in seven years. We have some way to go to match the team work of the Double side, but we're getting there. I'm particularly pleased for our skipper Dave Mackay, who has shown unbelievable determination to come back after twice breaking his leg. Many players in his position would have thrown in the towel, but Dave is made of special stuff.

The 1967 final may have been tame, but the shenanigans at the two after-match banquets kept we headline-hungry football reporters on our toes. The Chelsea players threatened to walk out on their 'celebration' dinner at the glitzy Carlton Tower Hotel in Belgravia in a row over their Cup final bonus. They claimed they had been promised £12,000 to be shared among the squad, but then learned on the eve of the match that they would be getting just £50-per-man.

Spurs held their dinner at the swanky Savoy Hotel in The Strand, but their directors fumed when most of the players left before the dessert to join the livelier party thrown by 'Super Fan' Morris Keston at the Hilton Hotel in Park Lane, where they had feasted four days before the final.

Morris, who has watched Spurs play home and away more than 3,000 times over a span of nearly 70 years, was friends with many of the players, for whom he organised lucrative testimonial matches and cash-raising events. The Tottenham directors, notoriously mean with their contracts, never forgave Keston for upstaging their banquet. But it didn't stop him still being considered 'Mr Tottenham' by the players, and he continued to get VIP treatment from them, while few directors were warmly welcomed in their company.

When I asked Bill Nick to comment on the behaviour of the players, he just shrugged and said: "I don't want to get involved. Suffice to say the directors felt they had been snubbed and insulted. It was a sad way to end a memorable day."

I'll tell you this, if Morris Keston had been running Spurs he would have doubled Bill Nicholson's wages and paid him what he was worth.

Three months later, Tottenham drew 3-3 in the Charity Shield against Manchester United at Old Trafford, a match that has gone down in footballing folklore because of a goal scored by Pat Jennings. The Irish international goalkeeper hammered a huge clearance from the Spurs penalty area that went first bounce over the head of Alex Stepney and into the back of the United net. The bewildered look on the faces of the players of both teams was hilarious to see.

I was reporting the match for the *Daily Express*, and afterwards Pat told me: "I decided to clear the ball up to Greavsie and Gilly, and a strong following wind grabbed it and took it all the way into the United net. Jimmy and Alan had their backs to me and could not believe it when they realized it was me who'd scored. Greavsie said he told Alan: 'D'you realise this makes Pat our top scorer? He'll never let us forget it.'"

The Greavsie era at Tottenham was drawing to a close, leaving a remarkable legacy of a club record 220 First Division goals (including a record 37 in 1962-63) and 32 FA Cup goals. Those bare statistics hide the fact that many of the goals were of the spectacular variety, fashioned like a skilled sculptor with clever feints, dizzying dribbles, astonishing acceleration and then finished with a pass rather than a shot into the net.

Those old enough to have witnessed a Greaves goal will confirm that I am not exaggerating when I say we actually felt privileged to have been there to see it. We were keeping company with a genius, a Goya of goals. How many would a peak-powered Greaves score in today's game, with no Norman Hunter-style bites-yer-legs tackling from behind and the relaxed, often-confusing off-side law? And what would he be worth in the transfer market? Let the bidding begin at £79,999,000!

There were calls for Greavsie to be reinstated in the England team when he hit a purple patch with 27 First Division goals in 1968-69, but Jimmy seemed to be almost visibly losing his appetite for the game the following season. Bill Nick told me privately that he was concerned that the Artful Dodger of the penalty area seemed to be showing more enthusiasm preparing for driving to Mexico in a 1970 World Cup rally than playing football. By this time, Jimmy had built up a flourishing sports shop and travel business with his brother-in-law Tom Barden, and football was no longer the be-all-and-end-all for him. Yet he was still by some distance the most dynamic finisher in the 'old' First Division. To try to bring the best out of Greavsie, Nicholson went shopping and bought Martin Chivers as a new playmate from Southampton.

How times change. In my reporting role for the *Daily Express* I met 'Big Chiv' at Waterloo Station and travelled with him by tube to Liverpool Street and then on to Tottenham as he prepared to start his new life at The Lane. These days, reporters cannot get near the prima donna players, who invariably arrive at their new clubs in chauffeur-driven limos with dark-tinted windows and shepherded by an agent handing out second-hand quotes.

Martin, a Grammar school boy educated at the highly regarded Taunton's School in Hampshire, spent the train journey from Southampton to Waterloo tackling *The Guardian* crossword. He told me on the way to The Lane: "This is like a dream for me. I've

SCRAPBOOK MEMORIES: *Jimmy Greaves was at home in Essex sweeping up in his new house on transfer deadline day in 1970 when he got a call from Bill Nicholson telling him of a different sort of move. He was off to West Ham in part-exchange for Martin Peters. In those days you had to guess the fees. It later emerged that this was the first £200,000 transfer, with Greavsie valued at £54,000.*

always been an admirer of the way Spurs play, and it's going to be a thrill as well as a challenge to play alongside Jimmy Greaves."

Sadly, he arrived at Jimmy's side just as the goal master was losing his motivation, and the very gentle giant was hardly helped by a knee injury that sidelined him for virtually an entire season. The crunch came when Spurs wore their white shirts like flags of surrender against Crystal Palace in a fourth round FA Cup replay at Selhurst Park. Palace striker Gerry Queen dismantled the Spurs defence for the winning goal, and I recall that the headline on my report for the *Daily Express* announced: "Queen Is King at the Palace."

Greavsie, struggling to settle to his partnership with Chivers, was dropped for the first time in his nine years at Spurs. It was his final curtain at Tottenham. On transfer deadline day in March 1970 Bill quietly arranged a swap deal that brought Martin Peters to White Hart Lane with Greavsie going to West Ham as a £54,000 makeweight in football's first £200,000 transfer deal. I have Greaves-besotted friends who surrendered their season tickets in protest.

Bill Nick, famous for his highly-polished shoes, military-short hair and trouser creases on which you could cut your fingers, had pulled off another very tidy transfer coup, without the media (including me) getting a sniff. He saw it as a two-edged deal:

●I was delighted to get Martin Peters, a player I'd admired for several years. But it was heartbreaking to have to let go of Jimmy, who was the greatest goalscorer I ever saw. But he had fallen out of love with the game, and sadly I was not far behind him, because the game was changing and not for the better. It had become ugly and defensive on the pitch and I despised the growing menace of hooliganism.●

The 1970s were about to provide Bill with his worst times in football. Author's warning: the following chapter is not for those Spurs fans of a nervous disposition.

Chapter Seven
*Souness and
Allotments*

WHILE my career took me to the *Daily Express* as chief football reporter via the London *Evening Standard* and the *Daily Herald* and then into television as a member of the *This Is Your Life* production team, Bill Nick buckled down to establishing himself as the greatest manager in the history of Spurs.

During these years of the Nicholson reign I wrote thousands of words about him and his teams, and I have the scrapbooks to prove it. We travelled to a dozen countries together, me as a member of the press brigade as we followed Spurs campaigning in Europe; also when Bill was acting as manager of the England Under-23 side on their summer tours.

It became a ritual that on the Sunday after home matches my late pal Harry Miller, of the *Daily Mirror*, and I would drop in on Bill at his Lane office. "Here they come," he would say with mock annoyance. "The terrible twins, Giller and Miller – songs at the piano. Got no time to talk, catching up with correspondence."

Then he would talk for an hour, and at the same time dragged any football gossip he could from Harry and me. People not in the game fail to realise that the English football scene is just a large village in which everybody knows everybody else and wants to know their neighbours' and rivals' business.

We rarely got a story we could print out of Bill, because he would always discipline himself to say, "This is off the record." But just to hear the wisest of men talking about the game he knew better than most was like sitting at the feet of an Einstein of football.

Bill lived just a short walk from the Lane in a modest three-bedroom end-of-terrace house at 71 Creighton Road. It was not in his nature to want the huge house and flash car trappings that usually come with success. Throughout his time at Tottenham and after the lifting of the maximum wage in 1961 he earned a lot less than his players. He was never ever motivated by profit, only League points and pots.

One particular Sunday Harry and I were standing listening to Bill on the edge of the pitch in a deserted stadium when we were interrupted by the tinkling of a bicycle bell. We looked up to find Grace Nicholson, Bill's wife, glowering at her husband.

Everybody called Grace Darkie, a nickname she had been given as a youngster to identify her from her fairer haired twin sister. She was a born smiler and I never ever found her less than friendly and charming, even when I was ringing Bill at home for late-night quotes on a breaking story. But this day she was clearly agitated.

"D'you know the time, Willie?" she called. "You're supposed to be taking the girls out."

Bill threw a hand to his head. "God, I completely forgot," he said. "Blame Giller and Miller. I'll be right home."

Darkie waved a friendly hand at Harry and me and then rode off, mission accomplished. She was a familiar figure locally as she rode her bike around the streets of Tottenham like a character out of a very English 1930s novel. Her bike was fitted with a shopping basket on the handlebars and she cycled to and from the stores and schools, where their daughters, Linda and Jean, were pupils. She was the woman behind (and often in front) of Bill, a loving, loyal wife in a blissfully happy marriage that lasted 62 years. Neither Darkie nor Bill – she usually called him Willie – were the slightest bit materialistic, and she was the perfect soccer wife who never stuck her nose into his business.

A former seamstress, Darkie was much more interested in teaching sewing at the local technical college than the Beautiful Game. Because the team tended to lose when she was watching, her superstitious husband insisted she kept away from the matches, and she used to follow home games by ear – judging how the team was doing by the decibels of the crowd roar through the kitchen window. Darkie being kept in the dark meant when Bill got home he could close the door on the football world that dominated all his thinking time away from his family.

By accident, I got an astonishing insight into the real Bill Nicholson. This was when he was overwhelmed by a story that made its way on to the front as well as back pages and which gave him more distress than almost any other event in his career.

It was during the 1970-71 season and Bill was losing a battle to hang on to one of the finest young prospects in British football, Graeme Souness. Born in the tough Broomhouse district of Edinburgh on May 6 1953, Graeme went to the same Carrickvale school that Dave Mackay had attended a generation earlier. They must have been hewn out of the identical lump of granite, because Souness had all the Mackay motivating mannerisms and liked to boss the pitch in the same intimidating way as his schoolboy idol.

His encyclopedic knowledge of all that Mackay achieved swayed him to join Tottenham at the age of fifteen when any of the Scottish clubs would willingly have opened their doors to him.

I learned earlier than most that Souness was not only a star in the making, but also a head-strong boy who knew his own mind. Jim Rodger, the sleuth of a reporter on the Scottish *Daily Express*, was so close to Bill Nicholson that he knew all the Spurs secrets and kept most of them tucked to his chest, never sharing them with readers or colleagues. He earned a mutual trust with chairmen, managers and players that got him an ear in boardrooms and dressing-rooms throughout football.

Jim, almost as wide as he was tall, was a legend in Scotland, on nodding terms with Prime Ministers and princes as well as most of the people who mattered in football. He telephoned me in the Fleet Street office of the *Express* one day in 1970 and whispered in the conspiratorial tone that he always used, 'Get over to the North London digs of Graeme Souness and talk him out of doing anything silly. Bill Nick thinks he's going to walk out on the club.'

'Graeme who?' I said. 'I wouldn't know what he looks like, let alone where he lives.'

'He's the hottest young prospect in the country,' Jim said in a scolding tone, and proceeded to give me Graeme's address. 'You'll be doing Bill Nick a big favour if you can tell him to just be patient and wait for his chance. He couldn't be with a better club. If you get him, put him on to me. I'll talk some sense into him.'

That was how 'Rodger the Dodger' operated, working almost as a secret agent on behalf of managers across Britain and then being rewarded with some of the hottest exclusive stories in the game.

In those days I was more concerned with trying to dig out stories on first-team players at all the London clubs, and could not see the point of chasing after a youngster whose career had hardly started. But as I had so much respect for my Glasgow colleague, I drove to Graeme's digs, only to be told by his landlady that he had gone home to Scotland an hour earlier.

'What a waste of time,' I thought. 'As if anybody apart from Jim Rodger is going to be the slightest bit interested in this story.' Wrong!

It got to the point over the next few days when questions were asked in the House of Commons, as the story crossed from the back to the front pages. Graeme, then seventeen, had spent two years at Spurs as an apprentice who considered himself more of a sorcerer. He had gone back to Edinburgh because he said he felt homesick.

Spurs reacted by suspending him without pay for two weeks. Graeme's local MP took up the case, and questioned in the House what right a club had to deal with 'a minor' like this when his only 'crime' was to suffer from homesickness. 'Is homesickness something that should be punishable?' demanded the MP, managing to make Souness sound as hard done by as Oliver Twist. The story became the target of columnists with poison pens, and Bill Nick, a fatherly manager if ever there was one, was unfairly pilloried. Souness, without having kicked a ball in senior football, was suddenly the best-known young player in the land.

The suspicion at Spurs was that their hot young property had been 'got at' and was being tempted away from Tottenham.

I went hunting Bill for quotes and found he had gone home from his Lane office. It was never my style to trouble managers by invading the privacy of their homes, but I was under pressure from my Editor to get a Nicholson slant on the story.

There was no reply when I knocked on his door and I was just about to return to my car when an elderly lady sweeping the pavement in front of her house next door said, "You looking for Mr Nicholson?"

I nodded, and she pointed to a side drive. "You'll find him around the back," she said. "He's in his allotment."

Allotment? Bill Nicholson, manager of Spurs? In his allotment?

Sure enough, I found Bill – dressed in shorts and Tottenham tracksuit top – digging with a spade in an allotment around the corner to his home.

"What the bloody hell do you want?" he said, as astonished to see me as I was to find him up to his ankles in shovelled soil.

"You spend a lot of time here?" I asked.

"I'd like to so that I could escape the likes of you," he replied, without a hint of humour. "One day I want to find more time to take it up as a proper hobby ... and if you say one word about it in your paper I will hang you from the nearest lamp-post."

I swore to secrecy and have never told this story until now, and I hope Bill Up There forgives me. I just feel it captures his (literally) down to earth personality. One of the nicest, kindest and most modest men ever to cross my path, but he could be brutal when necessary.

I pressed him for a response on Souness.

'I have never known such an ambitious and impatient young man,' an exasperated Nicholson told me, putting his spade aside. 'He has a wonderful future in the game, but he wants to run before he can walk. He can't understand why I'm not already considering him for the first-team. He wants to jump ahead of established professionals like Alan Mullery and Martin Peters, and the very promising Steve Perryman. His chance will come,

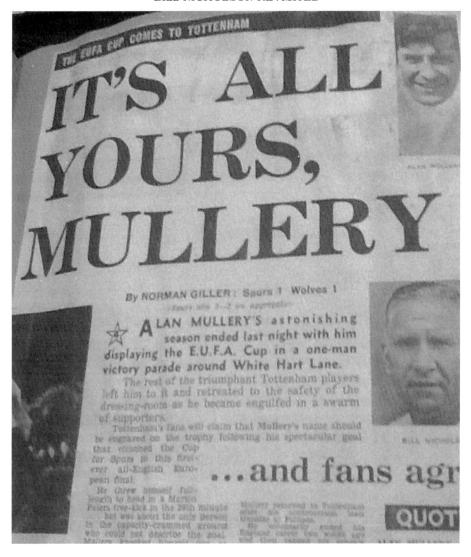

SCRAPBOOK MEMORIES: Alan Mullery performed a one-man lap of honour hugging the Uefa Cup after this draw against Wolves had given Spurs a victory on aggregate over the two legs. The celebrating crowd spilled on to the pitch, separating Mullery from his team-mates. Bill Nick angered his players by going into the Wolves dressing-room and commiserating with them and then rollocking his team for what he considered a below-standard performance.

but he must show patience. If he's ever picked for Scotland I wonder if they'll find a cap big enough for his head.'

A suitably repentant Souness returned to the Lane after Bill had travelled to Scotland to have quiet, fatherly words with him, but he wore out the carpet to Bill's office to the point where the Spurs boss decided he had no option but to let him go.

He had made one brief first-team appearance in a Uefa Cup tie (substituting for Martin Peters in a match in Iceland) before being sold to Middlesbrough in December 1972 for £27,000, which was a hefty fee in those days for a virtually unknown and untried player. Graeme went on to become one of the most formidable midfield forces in football, his peak coming when he joined Bob Paisley's Liverpool

For ever after, Bill 'Digger' Nicholson considered Souness 'the one that slipped through the net.'

DURING my fourteen years as a member of the *This Is Your Life* scriptwriting team, I was continually trying to get Bill Nicholson 'booked'. One of my roles was to prepare dossiers for the show's producer, Malcolm Morris, who would run them past Eamonn Andrews and, for the later series, Michael Aspel.

Sadly, a much deserved tribute never got past the programme planning stage. But at least this book gives me the chance to take a microscope to Bill's life and times.

One of the reasons the programme producers were nervous about featuring Bill was that his close confidante, Danny Blanchflower, had famously turned down Eamonn and told him politely where to stick his red book. It cost thousands to scrap the planned show, because relatives, clubmates and friends had been brought from all parts of the globe to join in a tribute to Danny Boy that never ever took place. The fear was that Bill – a shy, private man – might be tempted to "do a Danny."

As I'd learned from my first memorable meeting with him in 1958, Bill was very much a tracksuit manager, and only really content when at the Cheshunt training ground working on tactics and theories with his 'other family' – the players.

I have fished out the dossier I compiled for the eyes of Eamonn Andrews in 1981, and here it is in the original note form (the quotes were put in to give Eamonn a taste of what the guests might say). We had to give each proposed subject a codeword, because if ever it leaked out that a *Life* show was being planned it would be instantly shelved. These are my confidential notes, exactly as they dropped on to the desk of that legendary broadcaster, Eamonn Andrews:

TIYL BILL NICHOLSON DOSSIER
Suggested codeword: Cockerel

Summary: William Edward Nicholson, ex-footballer and later football manager: born Scarborough, Yorkshire, 26 January 1919; played for Tottenham Hotspur 1936-55, manager 1958-74, managerial consultant West Ham 1975-76; currently chief scout and consultant at White Hart Lane; capped once for England 1951; OBE 1975.

Personal: Married to Grace (known as Darkie). They have two daughters (Linda and Jean), and throughout his managerial career with Tottenham he and the family lived in an end of terrace house within walking distance of White Hart Lane. Darkie famously cycled to the local shops on a push bike. He banned her from watching them play because he considered her a Jonah.

Quote (circa 1970) from Darkie, a charming and bubbly lady: "I accept that Bill has two marriages – one to me, the other to football in general and Tottenham Hotspur in particular. Even when we are on summer holiday in Scarborough his mind is eaten up with ideas for the following season. Sometimes I wonder if he should have a bed put in his office at White Hart Lane!"

EARLY LIFE: Born and raised between the wars in Scarborough, the second youngest of a hansom-cab driver's nine children. Grew up during the Depression, and on leaving school at the

SCRAPBOOK MEMORIES: Darkie Nicholson would have loved to have gone to watch her husband's team play, but as I revealed in this 1972 feature Bill banned her because he considered her a Jonah. Darkie used to have her kitchen window open on home match days and judge how the game was going by the roars of the crowd.

age of 14, he took a job as a laundry boy and played his football for Scarborough Young Liberals and Scarborough Working Men's Club. In 1936, aged 16, he was spotted by Spurs and moved south to join their nursery club, Gravesend and Northfleet, before turning professional in 1938. Best person to cover this part of his footballing life is Ronnie Burgess, who captained Spurs and Wales in the 1950s and was Bill's close pal.

Quote (circa 1961) from Ron Burgess: "Bill was the most conscientious footballer I ever played with. He gave 100 per cent in everything that he did, and would always put the team first. In those early days at Gravesend and then in the first-team he unselfishly agreed to play at left-back, even though he was essentially right footed. He lost his best years to the war, otherwise he would have won a load of England caps."

WAR YEARS: Bill had just started to establish himself in the first-team when war was declared in September 1939. He served in the Durham Light Infantry, stationed mainly in England – first as an infantry instructor, then a physical training instructor – and found time for Saturday wartime League guest appearances with Middlesbrough, Sunderland, Newcastle United and Darlington. When he reported back to Spurs in 1945 he first of all played at centre-half and then switched to right-half, the position in which he was to establish himself as one of the most reliable and industrious players in the League. He became a key man in the Spurs 'Push and Run' team that in back-to-back seasons of 1949 to 1951 won the Second Division and First Division titles.

Note to Eamonn: Ideally we should bring in Alf Ramsey here, but he always refuses to do the show. I think he is in fear that he will be the subject, and likes to keep his gypsy background private. Instead, we can go for Push and Run schemer Eddie Baily

Quote (circa 1967) from Eddie Baily, England and Tottenham inside-left and later coach, who was nicknamed the Cheeky

Chappie after comedian Max Miller: "Bill was a players' player. He did not hunt personal glory but gave everything he had to the team. You could count his bad games on the fingers of One Arm Lou (a notorious ticket spiv of the time). The Push and Run side would not have functioned nearly so well without Billy's energy and enthusiasm. He covered for Alf behind him and prompted the forwards with neat rather than spectacular passes. He left those to me! He learned a lot from our great manager Arthur Rowe, and when he retired it was obvious he would make an outstanding coach and manager. He was a born tactician."

PLAYING CAREER: Bill played 314 League games for Spurs as a defensive midfield player, and scored six goals. He won one England cap for England as stand-in for injured Billy Wright – against Portugal at Goodison in May 1951 when he was 32. Remarkably, he scored with his first kick in international football, netting from 20 yards with a drive in the first minute. He never got another call-up because of the consistency of Billy Wright.

Quote (circa 1980) from Billy Wright, England and Wolves captain, former Arsenal manager and now Head of Sport at ATV: "Typical of Bill, when I told him he had deserved another chance with England he said, 'No, you're the better player and the No 4 England shirt belongs to you.' I have rarely known such a modest man, and he is the perfect role model for young players coming into the game and also young managers. I may have been a better player, but it was no race as to which of us was the better manager! He was one of the top three in the game. His coaching ability was second to none, full of invention and creativity."

THE COACH: In 1954, Bill was honest enough to admit that his troublesome knee would not allow him to play at full power any more and he voluntarily stood down from the team and after helping the reserves for a while retired to concentrate on his first love of coaching. He gained his FA coaching badge at the first attempt and worked with the Tottenham youth squad and also with the Cambridge University team. In 1957 he became assistant to manager Jimmy Anderson, who had replaced the unwell Arthur Rowe. In 1958 he was a member of the coaching staff that travelled to Sweden for the World Cup finals.

Quote (circa 1968) from Sir Walter Winterbottom, England manager 1947-1962 and later chairman of the Central Council for Physical Recreation: "I assigned Bill to watch the Brazilians durng the 1958 games in readiness for our match. He came back with his head full of tactical plans, and we sat down and worked out how we could stop a team that was beating everybody in sight. It was largely due to Bill's creative input that we held Brazil to a goalless draw. It was an extraordinary performance against a team that became arguably the greatest world champions ever. Bill has proved beyond question that he is one of the most astute managers and coaches our game has ever produced."

Bill juggled his Tottenham manager's role with taking charge of the England Under-23 summer tours for many years, and was the choice of a lot of good judges to take over the England job before his old Tottenham team-mate Alf Ramsey was made manager in 1962, after Nick had made it clear he was not interested.

THE CLUB MANAGER: In October 1958, Bill was appointed manager in place of Jimmy Anderson and on the very day that he took charge Spurs beat Everton 10-4! The star of the match was 'Tom Thumb' Tommy Harmer, who scored one goal and helped created seven others ...

Quote (circa 1980) from Tommy Harmer, Tottenham's tiny tot midfield schemer, a chain-smoker and now a messenger in the City: "It was one of those matches when everything we touched turned to goals. It could easily have been 15-8!

When we came off at the end I said to Bill, 'Don't expect this every week, Boss.' He was always like a big brother to me."

The greatest feat with which Bill will always be associated was the League and FA Cup Double of 1960-61, the first time it had been achieved n the 20th Century and considered the 'Impossible Dream.' Bill and his captain Danny Blanchflower were the driving force that lifted Tottenham into the land of legend. Many experts rate that Double team the greatest British club side of all time.

Note to Eamonn: The perfect person to produce here would be Danny, but after your previous experience I am sure you will not second that opinion! So I suggest Dave Mackay, the heart of the Spurs ...

Quote (circa 1980) from Dave Mackay: "Bill was a master tactician, who could see a game in his mind before it was played. He had a photographic memory when it came to footballers, and could recall instantly the strengths and weaknesses of almost any player he had ever seen. I considered myself fortunate to play under him and tried to take his attitude and application into management."

The summer after completing the Double, Bill went to Italy and bought Jimmy Greaves from AC Milan for £99,999 (not wanting to give Jimmy the pressure of being the first £100,000 footballer). That following season Spurs won the FA Cup and reached the semi-finals of the European Cup, going out in controversial circumstances to eventual champions Benfica. This should be when we spring Jimmy Greaves (with whom I am currently writing our sixth book together):

Quote (1981) from Jimmy Greaves: "Bill would not be my choice as company for a night out on the town, but he would be first on my list of managers. He can be dour and tunnel visioned where football is concerned, but he does not see his job to be a comedian. His teams always entertain on the pitch, and that's because he gives them free rein. He never tried to put any restrictions on me and I enjoyed the freedom. We won the FA Cup for Bill in 1962, which was consolation for not beating Benfica in the European Cup semi-final. I had a perfectly good goal ruled off-side, which would have given us a chance of reaching the final."

The following season Tottenham created history by becoming the first team to win a major European trophy, with a 5-1 victory over Atletico Madrid in the European Cup Winners' Cup final in Rotterdam. We could have fun here by bringing on Bill's big pal Bill Shankly ...

Quote (circa 1973) from Bill Shankly, legendary Liverpool manager: "Bill is the canniest manager in the business, who always comes up with tactical thoughts that make the difference between winning and losing. He showed us all the way to win in Europe, and has set standards that we are all trying to match. I have enormous respect for him as a manager and as a man."

In less than a year Nicholson lost the engine room of his dream team. Skipper Danny Blanchflower retired with a knee injury, the swashbuckling Dave Mackay suffered a twice-broken leg, and John White was tragically killed when struck by lightning on a golf course. Bill set about rebuilding his side and brought in Pat Jennings from Watford, Cyril Knowles from Middlesbrough, Alan Mullery from Fulham, Mike England from Blackburn, Alan Gilzean from Dundee and Terry Venables from Chelsea.

Quote (circa 1980) from Terry Venables: "It was close to an impossible job to follow in the footsteps of that great Double side. That is the sort of team that comes along only once in a lifetime. But we did our best and managed to win the FA Cup in 1967. Bill set the benchmarks for all future Tottenham managers."

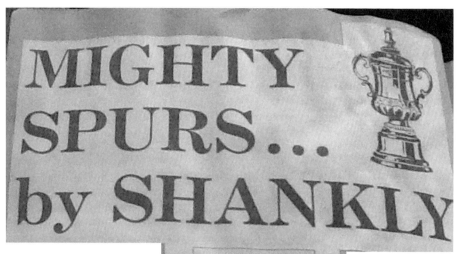

By NORMAN GILLER

BILL SHANKLY gave me a remarkable analysis last night of the Tottenham team his Liverpool Lions face at Anfield on Saturday.

Shanks—the James Cagney of Soccer—gave Spurs the sort of verbal build-up he usually hoards exclusively for Liverpool.

And he made Tottenham's Bill Nicholson sound the greatest manager of all time.

"When I praise Spurs and boost Shanks...

This is Shanks on Nicholson.

"Bill is a one's a man's man, who thinks big and acts big. He has the courage of his own convictions but never shouts about his great achievements."

Exclusive League

"Bill Nicholson has a special place in my private Hall of Fame. He belongs to my exclusive League of Trustworthy Men.

"Notice I do not say League of Gentlemen. It's no use trying to be a gentleman in this world. You'll just get spat on.

"This is a cut-throat business full of people who want to cut your throat..."

SCRAPBOOK MEMORIES: *Here's proof why Bill Shankly would have been the perfect walk-on guest in a Bill Nicholson* This Is Your Life *programme. Shanks and Bill were good friends with a mutual respect for each other's football knowledge. They shared the belief that the Beautiful Game should be played with skill as the main plank, and both practised what they preached. British managers who were proud of their British players. The good old days.*

There were victories in the the League Cup (1971 and 1973) and the Uefa Cup (1972), but Nicholson set his targets high and – disillusioned by the pay demands of several of his players, and hooliganism among a section of the supporters – he resigned in 1974, but was coaxed back in a consultancy capacity by manager Keith Burkinshaw after a brief interlude at West Ham

He was rewarded with an OBE for his services to football, while most in the game and certainly the Tottenham supporters feel he should have been given a knighthood.

As a surprise guest at the end of the show I suggest we spring Arthur Rowe, manager of the Push and Run Spurs who was a huge influence on Bill both as a player and as a coach. Bill will be thrilled to see him.

That was my dossier to Eamonn, but the show producers decided that Bill had led a too one-dimensional football-football-football life, and the risk of him saying 'no' was too great.

It was heartbreaking for those of us close to Bill to witness him losing his enthusiasm for the job that had been his life. It was a mixture of the hooliganism of the 1970s and the growing greed of the players that made him fall out of love with the game at the age of 55. I remember Bill describing the night that Tottenham played Feyenoord in Rotterdam in the second leg of the Uefa Cup final on May 29 1974 as "the saddest night of my life" It was what happened off the pitch rather than on it, where Spurs were soundly beaten 2-0 to give Feyenoord a 4-2 aggregate victory.

The Uefa Cup had been the exclusive property of Football League clubs for six successive years, but Feyenoord deservedly became the first Dutch winners of the trophy after a final that turned into the blackest event in Tottenham's proud history.

Spurs had been flattered by a 2-2 draw in the first leg at White Hart Lane. A goal just before half-time from centre-half Mike England and an own goal by Van Daele cancelled out goals by the highly skilled tandem team of Van Hanegem and De Jong.

Feyenoord were comfortably the better team in the second-leg, and a section of so-called Spurs supporters could not stomach seeing their team being made to look strictly second best.

The Dutch masters clinched victory with their second goal two minutes from the final whistle. This sparked a riot by Spurs followers that led to 70 arrests and to 200 spectators being treated for injuries.

Bill Nicholson, choking back tears, appealed over the public address system for sanity. "You hooligans are a disgrace to Tottenham Hotspur and a disgrace to England," he said. "This is a game of football – not a war."

That night Bill Nick was close to walking out on his beloved Tottenham. He said in an emotional after-match statement:

"This is a heartbreaking night for football in general and Tottenham in particular. It makes you wonder if it is all worth it when you see people behaving like animals. It is not just a football problem. It is a social problem, and hooliganism is eating into our great game. Questions should be asked as to whether there is enough discipline in homes and schools. Feyenoord were worthy winners, and I am extremely embarrassed that a minority among our supporters – people we should disown – were unable to accept the fact that we were beaten by a better side."

Bill's departure was delayed just a few months. He festered and fretted throughout the summer, waiting for the new season for the first time in his career without enthusiasm. He felt the club had been badly wounded by the incident in Rotterdam, and he was disillusioned by the way widespread hooliganism was scarring the face of the once Beautiful Game.

He had suddenly lost the ability to motivate his players, and he slipped into a deep depression as Spurs got off to their worst start ever with four successive defeats. Bill felt exhausted.

On August 29 1974, 'Mr Tottenham' handed in his resignation, bringing to an end 39 years service to the club and 16 of them as the most successful manager in Spurs history.

It was not only hooliganism that had robbed Nicholson of his appetite, but also player power and greed. He revealed: "Players

SCRAPBOOK MEMORIES: One of the main reasons Bill fell out of love with his job as manager was a continual battle with his players over contracts. He saw it as galloping greed, while the players argued they were only trying to get what they thought they were worth.

have become impossible. They talk all the time about security, but they are not prepared to work for it. I am abused by players when they come to see me. There is no longer respect ..."

It was widely reported that Martin Chivers was the player giving Nick the biggest headache with his attitude. Coach Eddie Baily said on the record: "He has got such a big head it's a wonder he can get through the dressing-room door. Somebody needs to teach him and a few of the other players the meaning of respect."

Bill Nick dropped a bombshell at a press conference by divulging: "I have recently found it impossible to get the players I want because at Tottenham we pride ourselves in not making under-the-counter payments. It is expected in the London area for players to ask for £7,000 tax free. That's the minimum asking price. I want no part of that world."

Skipper Martin Peters, Pat Jennings and Phil Beal made a private visit to Nicholson on behalf of the players to ask him to change his mind but he said there was no going back.

The Tottenham directors wrung their hands, and allowed the Master of White Hart Lane to leave, when an arm around the shoulders and warm words of encouragement could have made him change his mind.

Eddie Baily, another long-time Spurs servant and a highly regarded and sometimes acid-tongued coach, departed with Nicholson, complaining loudly about what he considered miserly contract-settlement terms. Bill Nick got a 'golden' handshake that he confidentially described to me as "pathetic."

Many years later Eddie confided that he had collected a laughable £4,000, while Bill Nick walked off with a cheque for £10,000 after 16 years in charge, during which the teams he built earned Spurs millions.

There were loud whispers that Lane icon Danny Blanchflower would take over. This is what Bill Nicholson had advised, but he found the directors deaf to his suggestions.

Instead, the Board appointed another Irishman, who had Arsenal stamped all the way through him. Terry Neill, a hero of Highbury, took over and, inevitably, it ended in tears.

Chapter Eight
Danny, the first Special One

T O write the Bill Nicholson story without reference to his special relationship with Danny Blanchflower would be like penning the tale of McCartney and forgetting to mention Lennon. An exaggeration? Possibly, but then Bill always did accuse me of writing fairy stories instead of telling the stark truth. "Tell it as it is," he used to admonish, "not how you would like it to be. You're not Hans Christian Anderson, you know. Stick to the facts."

Bill and Danny were not just manager and captain. To listen to them talking tactics was like being in on a strategy meeting between two army field marshals, plotting the upcoming game as if it were a military campaign.

They got off to a rocky start when Bill first took over as manager. He considered Danny too cavalier a player, and dropped him because he felt his all-out attacking policy was not right for the team. Bill had traced that many of the goals Spurs were leaking in his first season were because Danny was not concentrating on his defensive duties.

Bill told me some years later when able to look back with an evaluation not weighed down by emotion:

•It was not an easy decision to make. You have to remember Danny had been bought from Aston Villa to replace me at the end of my career, and so it could have looked as if I was dropping him just to show I was boss. But that was never my style.

"In a way I wanted to teach Danny a lesson. He was one of the finest attacking midfield players of all time, but he was letting the team down by not seeming to care what his opposing inside-forward was doing.

SCRAPBOOK MEMORIES: This is the headline thousands of Spurs fans would liked to have seen. i wrote the story in 1971 after discussing the idea with Everton boss Harry Catterick, but the message did not get through to the Establishment. Bill got the consolation of an OBE. But it should have been a knighthood.

"He felt that I was trying to send him signals that his career was over. He was 33 and troubled by niggling knee injuries. That was not the case at all. I just wanted him to take a look at his game, but he misunderstood and asked for a transfer.

"There was no way I was going to let him go. I saw him as the ideal captain for us, provided he became more of a team player. He took my point, came back into the team, tightened his defensive play and became the most inspirational captain I had ever seen.'

Nicholson and Blanchflower became so closely knit that you could have thought they were joint managers. Danny, a walking, talking quotes machine, was more prominent in the press than Bill, who was reticent to make too many bold statements in case they came back to bite him.

Bill always shunned personal publicity, and would wince when he saw the new cult developing of managers taking a stage that once belonged exclusively to the players. He used to be at his most articulate in defeat, cutting down any players he felt were getting an inflated opinion of their own ability. In victory, he was content to let his team's performance do the talking for him.

He could be savagely candid, and never gave praise that had not been earned. His players found his compliments hard to come by because he was a perfectionist, who demanded the highest level of performance at all times. He was not interested enough in self-projection as a manager to earn the public's affection, but in the autumn of his life – after being reinstated at the club following a clumsily handled end to his managerial career – he became the father figure at Tottenham, and was warmly regarded by everybody who had close contact with him during those 'Glory, Glory' days.

There is still a campaign going on to get him a posthumous knighthood, for which he was shamefully overlooked during his life. But all those well-intentioned petitioners are wasting their time and energy. If they give one to Bill Nick, what do they do about the likes of Bill Shankly, Bob Paisley, Arthur Rowe, Jock

Stein, Stan Cullis, Billy Wright, Bobby Moore ... I could go on and on. Bill would have hated the fuss. He liked things to be low key.

Danny on the other hand loved the limelight, provided it did not shine on his rather complicated private life that took in three marriages and generated the sort of tittle-tattle gossip that he despised. He confided in me that the main reason he turned down the *This Is Your Life* tribute is that he was deep into an affair and about to tell his then wife that he wanted a divorce.

It had been the summer of 1960 when the eloquent Irishman told veteran Tottenham chairman Fred Bearman: "We're going to win the League for you this coming season, Mr Chairman, and for good measure we will throw in the FA Cup, too."

The elderly Spurs boardroom boss could be forgiven for thinking it was a piece of Blanchflower blarney. He was often using his wit and imagination to embroider stories until they were into fairyland. Mr Bearman was older than the century, and he knew better than most that the League and Cup double had become football's "impossible dream"

It had been beyond the reach of Herbert Chapman's great pre-war Arsenal and Huddersfield teams, too difficult a target for an Everton side fuelled by the goals of Dixie Dean and then Tommy Lawton, and a bridge too far for the smooth, sophisticated Spurs Push and Run side of the early 1950s. And just in the previous three years the Stan Cullis Wolves and then Matt Busby's Manchester United had got within shooting distance of the two supreme prizes, only to fall at the final hurdle.

Mr Bearman wanted to believe his club captain but must have harboured deep doubts. Superstitious Spurs supporters, buoyed by the fact that there was a '1' in the upcoming year, also wanted to believe that a major trophy was coming their way. The League championship? Possibly. The FA Cup? Maybe. Both of them? Not a hope. The build-up involved in trying to capture the two trophies needed such contrasting preparations that it was too easy to fall between the two and finish empty-handed.

The race for the League title was a marathon that called for stamina, consistency, and a total commitment to trying to win week in and week out. The FA Cup was like a sudden-death sprint through a minefield with no knowing what explosions waited around the corner. The tripwire could be hidden at such unfashionable soccer outposts as Walsall (ask Arsenal), Bournemouth (ask Manchester United and Spurs), Yeovil (ask Sunderland), or Worcester (ask Liverpool). No team in the 20th Century had achieved the elusive double, but Danny Blanchflower was *not* joking. He was quietly insisting that it could be done, and set about convincing anybody in earshot at White Hart Lane during the build-up to the season. As he spoke from a position of responsibility and influence in his role as Spurs captain he had to be listened to, but few really shared his belief at the start of what was to become an historic 1960-61 season.

Bill Nicholson also quietly believed it, but unlike Danny Boy he kept it to himself. He once told me: "Your tongue can get you into much more trouble than your toes." Yes, a wise man.

It was in midfield where Spurs won most matches in that Double season thanks to the combination of skill and strength springing from skipper Blanchflower, schemer John White and thunder-tackler Dave Mackay. Blanchflower was the poet of the side, Mackay the buccaneering pirate, and White the prince of passers.

The day he collected the FA Cup at Wembley, Danny tried to get Bill to join in the lap of honour around the Wembley pitch. "Come on, Bill," he said. "This is as much your triumph as ours."

"No," said Bill, "this day belongs to the players and our supporters."

Arrogance and Bill Nicholson were complete strangers. His next boast would be his first.

Fast forward five years, and Danny and I became team-mates with *Express* newspapers in the days when I was chief football reporter for the *Daily* and Danny the thought-provoking columnist for the *Sunday*. We remained good pals after I had tunnelled my way out of Fleet Street to become an author (pretentious, moi?) and a freeelance television scriptwriter and newspaper contributor. One of my roles was *The Judge* of *The Sun*, answering readers' questions and settling pub arguments. One day I received a question that read: "If the job offer came along, would Danny Blanchflower consider returning to football as manager of Spurs?"

Danny, who could be witty, wise and weird in equal measure and all within one thought process, prided himself on never ducking a question, but on this occasion he was unusually prickly.

"All right, what do you know?" he asked. "I'm sworn to secrecy."

Purely by coincidence I had stumbled on a developing story of major proportions.

"This is a genuine question from a reader," I told him. "What's going on?"

There was a long silence, which was a rare thing when talking to Danny, because he liked to fill every waking moment with original ideas and unique observations. To wind him up, I used to call him Danny Blarneyflower.

"I don't want to tell you on the telephone," he said, mysteriously. "Meet me at the Alex Forbes café in half an hour."

This was a coffee house near Blackfriars' Station, a short walk from Fleet Street. It was years since it had been owned by former Arsenal star Alex Forbes but was still known to football journos by his name. It was the sort of nondescript place where you could melt into the background while meeting contacts.

There was a touch of a John Le Carré spy thriller about Danny's entrance into the coffee house. He was looking around furtively as if making sure he had not been followed.

"What's with all the cloak and dagger stuff?" I asked.

Danny was obviously agonizing. "I'm going to have to ask you to give me your word that all I am about to tell you is confidential," he said. "You're going to be desperate to break the story, but because I cannot tell a lie I'm going to take you into my confidence.

If it leaks, it could stop me getting a job I have always dreamed about – manager of Spurs."

I spluttered into my coffee cup. "You've known me long enough to realise you can trust me," I said. "Thank goodness I'm not a staff reporter any more. My duty then would be to the newspaper."

"And then I wouldn't be telling you," said Danny, with his usual good reasoning. "The fact is that Bill Nick is on the point of resigning from Spurs, and he wants to put my name forward as his successor."

The newspaperman in me was aching to get that sensational story into print, but Danny had tied me into a straitjacket of secrecy.

"When you rang me and asked that question as The Judge, I thought it was your crafty way of saying you were on to the story," he explained. "Bill confided in me a week ago what he was planning, and I have been trying to talk him out of it. I've never known him so low and so lacking in appetite for the game that has been his life. He is completely disillusioned with football, or the politics of it. Bill doesn't like what he sees with the galloping greed of the players, and the violence on the terraces has sickened him. I said that perhaps he was trying to pass me a poisoned chalice."

It was a month before Nicholson's stunning decision to quit became public, and the veteran manager made no secret of the fact that he wanted Tottenham icon Danny Blanchflower to take over from him. He had even teed-up ex-Leeds playmaker Johnny Giles as player-coach.

The board made a complete botch of it, and decided instead to hand the reins to Danny's fellow Irishman Terry Neill, a man with Arsenal-red blood. They were frightened that Blanchflower would dictate to them, as he would have done.

"It can only end in tears," Danny told me privately. "Terry is an intelligent man with lots of bright ideas, but he has as much chance of being accepted at Tottenham as the Archbishop of Canterbury has of being welcomed at the Vatican."

It's history, of course, that Danny did eventually come back

Why he decided to quit

DANNY'S DREAM ENDS

DISILLUSIONED Danny Blanchflower yesterday quit Chelsea because he cannot come to terms with the game's values.

Blanchflower admitted his reasons for leaving after nine months as manager were more to do with conscience than contracts.

He said: "I always said I would go when the time was right. I think that moment has come."

"The club now need to appoint a younger man more in touch with the values of the game—particularly off the field."

And he added, significantly: "There is no way I could pay £1 million for a fair to average player, which is the going rate, without it weighing on my conscience. I am too old to change my beliefs.

"I know the board here think nearer to my values than the game does. I have been trying to persuade the two or three months that I should give way.

PICTURE : LEONARD TRIEVNOR

Blanchflower yesterday ... the last exit from his Bridge of sighs

SPORTS OPINION

Sad—but it had to be . . .

DANNY BLANCHFLOWER'S departure from Chelsea is sad —but it was almost inevitable. His strength was always as the grand strategist; what Chelsea need is a commando sergeant—a man who will eat, sleep and breathe with his men during the dangers ahead. Blanchflower speaks more sense than most people in the game. But it's a comment on the over-competitiveness of the modern era that there is really no place for him in club management.

Perhaps he sat too long on the sidelines and when he finally stepped back into the fray, the generation gap was too great.

His vision, spirit of adventure and concepts were essentially geared to better players than were ever available to him at Chelsea and he was adrift in the middle range of the transfer market.

Outburst

"But he was reluctant. When I read Peter Osgood's outburst at the weekend about the gap in thinking between myself and some of the players I approached Brian again.

"What is needed here to get the club back in the First Division is a three to four-year job which a

'Chelsea need a young manager'

Mears underlined there will be no quick appointment, admitting : "We have to get it right this time. We have a board meeting tomorrow. I'm very disappointed that Danny is going."

Geoff Hurst, appointed coach at the start of the season will almost definitely select the side this weekend —but with no guarantee of getting the job on a permanent basis.

Blanchflower, 52, will now

team, his sports journalism and playing golf.

Since sacking Dave Sexton in 1974 Chelsea have had caretaker managers in Ron Suart and Frank Upton. And they have had permanent men in Eddie McCreadie, Ken Shellito, and Blanchflower.

Blanchflower, however, made it clear this was never meant to be a long-term venture.

He said : "Chelsea are a unique club. It is a social as well as a football club

SCRAPBOOK MEMORIES: Danny's real dream was to manage Tottenham, but he found himself in charge at Stamford Bridge, and it became a nine-month nightmare. Chelsea won only five of the 32 games under his management. He later admitted to me that his big chance to manage at the top had come too late, and he found it difficult to motivate the players. Danny would have preferred to work with the previous generation ... and players wearing the Lilywhite colours of Tottenham that he wore with such pride and passion.

into football – as manager of Chelsea; which made as much sense as Terry Neill being appointed boss at White Hart Lane.

It was a total disaster that could be measured on the Richter Scale. Chelsea won only five of 32 matches on their way to relegation in 1978-79, and a completely humiliated Blanchflower threw in the towel after just nine months in charge. Truly, a Bridge too far.

"Right place, wrong time," Danny told me, fighting to hide his disappointment and disillusionment. "Suddenly I found myself not being able to talk the same language as the players. I thought I was making sense, but they couldn't understand me and were unable to translate what I was trying to convey into action on the pitch. I tried to take the Bill Nicholson route, keeping things simple. But even when I was A-B-C-ing it they did not get the message. It dawned on me that there was too big an age difference between me and the players. It needs a younger manager to get hold of them and motivate them. Ten years ago it would have been a different story. We talked a different language then. The game has changed out of sight."

Danny and the Beautiful Game that he had played so beautifully had become passing strangers.

I interviewed Danny in happier times in 1971, getting him to compare the Tottenham Double-winning side with the Arsenal team that completed the League and FA Cup double exactly ten years after Danny had led Spurs to the historic "couple." I feel justified in repeating his choices here because he is talking about the team that Bill Nicholson built.

These were his considered man by man ratings:

Bill Brown v Bob Wilson: "Not a lot to choose between them. Bill used to give me grey hairs with some of his positioning, but he had a good safe pair of hands and never let the side down. Wilson has made enormous improvement, and is now just a fingertip ahead of Bill in all-round goalkeeper skills. So I select Bob, but he is not in the same class as Pat Jennings."

Peter Baker v Pat Rice: "I often felt guilty about taking my wages because Peter did so much covering behind me. I had a dodgy knee in my last three seasons at Tottenham, and I would not have been nearly as effective without Peter working so hard. Pat is a good, solid and reliable right-back but my conscience insists I give the nod to Peter."

Bob McNab v Ron Henry: "Ron was greatly under-estimated, and deserved more than his solitary cap for England. He had good ball control, and could tackle with venom. Bobby McNab is a tigerish player who uses the ball intelligently, and just edges out Ron in my opinion.."

Danny Blanchflower v. Peter Storey: "As if I'm not going to select myself! Accuse me of many things, but not false modesty. With respect to Peter, he doesn't have my experience which meant I could dictate matches not only with my passing but with my thinking. It strikes me Peter is played mainly in a destructive role. He does it efficiently but it's too negative for my taste."

Maurice Norman v Frank McLintock: "Frank and I had the captain's responsibility in common, and I think it fair to say we were both key players for our team. Of course, Frank was right-half in the Leicester team we beat to clinch the Double in the FA Cup final. He has switched to centre-half with impressive skill and determination, and – while Maurice had a distinct edge in the air – I would have to pick Frank to fill the No 5 shirt."

Dave Mackay v Peter Simpson: Sorry, but this is no race. Peter is one of the most consistent defenders in the country, but he is not in the same League as Dave Mackay. If I was picking a world eleven, Dave would be one of my first choices. He energised the team, frightened the life out of the opposition and had exceptional skill to go with his strength.

Cliff Jones v George Armstrong. We are talking world class – Cliff – against a good-quality domestic player. Cliff had the speed, the skill and the courage to take apart the tightest defence. His bravery was beyond belief and he used to make me shudder the way he would dive in where others feared to tread. George is a fine creative winger but not in the same league as Jones. We are talking one of the greatest wingers the UK has ever produced.

John White v George Graham. Again, this is no race. John was the hidden ace in our team, making it tick with his measured passes and opening the way to goal with clever blind-side running. George has good skills and is a player of vision, but the inventive John White was a class above him. He was a joy to play with and was always popping up in the right place to collect a pass. But for his tragically early death, I am convinced John would have written himself much larger into football's hall of fame.

Bobby Smith v John Radford. At his peak in that Double year, Bobby broke down the best defences in the land with his battering-ram strength and explosive finishing. He was not all raw power, but had deceptive changes of pace and excellent close control. People used to find it hard to believe that he stood only 5ft 9in tall. John is a determined player with good positional sense and a deft touch in front of goal, but you ask any centre-half whom he would least like to mark out of Smith and Radford and I guarantee they would all go for the Tottenham man.

Les Allen v Ray Kennedy. Les was the perfect partner for Bobby Smith in that Double season, playing with subtlety and skill that balanced Bobby's strength. He was unlucky to lose his place the following season to the one and only Jimmy Greaves (we are talking genius). Ray Kennedy is a strong, willing and promising player but has some way to go before he can be considered as effective as Allen.

Terry Dyson v Charlie George. Our Mr Dependable, Terry could be counted on to run himself into the ground for the team. But going on potential and promise, I am giving Charlie George the final place. He is an outstanding prospect, and has natural finishing skills that you cannot teach. He has that natural ability to be able to do the unexpected. In football, that is a priceless gift.

So Danny Boy's combined 'Doubles' team lined up like this (in 4-2-4 formation):

Bob Wilson

Peter Baker Frank McLintock Dave Mackay Bob McNab

Danny Blanchflower   John White

Cliff Jones Bobby Smith Les Allen Charlie George

Inevitably, I asked Danny who he would have managing the team out of Bill Nicholson or Bertie Mee.

"That is the easiest choice of all," he said. "Bertie Mee is a master organiser, excellent at man management and supreme at delegation, but he is not in the same street as Bill Nicholson when it comes to football management.

"Yes, Mee's Arsenal have just become the second team after Spurs to win the League and Cup double this century, but come on – I know I'm biased, but they were not fit to tie the boot laces of Bill's Double team.

"I would put Bill in the very top bracket of managers along with the likes of Matt Busby and Bill Shankly. He has a vast knowledge of the game at all levels, is a genius of a tactician and is the most honest man I have ever met. An absolute diamond."

I so wish there was a happy ending to this Danny Blanchflower Revisited tale, but – as Danny would say – it ended in tears. When I went to see him in 1991 for a thirtieth anniversary chat about the Double year I was devastated to find he could barely remember the name of a single player.

He was into the early stages of the Alzheimer's Disease that tragically made the last few years of his life a blank before he passed on in 1993, aged 67.

Bill Nicholson unashamedly shed tears when he heard of Blanchflower's passing. "Danny was a romantic who believed anything and everything was possible," he said. "I envied him his imagination and his wonderful wit. He was quite comfortably the finest captain I had ever seen, and I just know he would have made an excellent manager of Spurs if he had been given the chance. But I think the Board were frightened of him. He was too bright for them. He could out-think the lot of them. The lot of us. He is irreplaceable."

In his peak years, Danny was one of the most skilful and certainly most intelligent footballers I ever had the pleasure to watch and write about. It was a privilege to be able to call him a friend and colleague. He is the subject of my next book: *Oh Danny Boy, This WAS Your Life*. See page 208

Before his memory was cruelly wiped, he told me: "I was so lucky to play for the greatest team and greatest manager the English game has known."

And those of us of a certain age were so lucky to have watched him playing for Spurs in those Glory-Glory days. My Danny Boy lament seems appropriate here:

Oh Danny Boy, the Spurs, the Spurs, are calling
From stand to stand and down the Shelf side
The summer's gone but memories are flying
Of glory-glory days that have never died.
But come ye back when the pitch is in meadow
Or when the Lane is hushed and white with snow
'Tis we'll be there in sunshine and in shadow
Oh Danny Boy, oh Danny Boy, we miss you so

Chapter Nine
The One That Got Away

BACK in the 1960s Spurs were known by sneering rival supporters as a Chequebook Club. There is evidence to support the accusations. For eight or more years Bill set the pace in the transfer market, continually beating the British record when bringing in the likes of Dave Mackay, Jimmy Greaves, Martin Chivers, Mike England, Martin Peters, Ralph Coates – all for what were then Football League record fees.

But there was method in Bill's apparent extravagance. He told me that each April he would meet with the club directors and accountants and it would be worked out how much should be spent to off-set against tax. So it was the accountants working on tax avoidance who decided how much should be spent each year.

As well as being an exceptional coach and manager, Bill was a master negotiator and rarely failed to get his man. His toughest negotiation was when bringing Greavsie back from Milan. Chelsea were also bidding and the Italians tried to play Spurs and Chelsea off against each other. But Bill was too astute for them.

He had a 'deepthroat' in the Chelsea club who told him that the maximum they were prepared to pay to get Greavsie back to where he started his career was £96,000.

When he got to Milan Bill contacted John Battersby, who was in Italy conducting the deal for Chelsea in his role as club secretary. "Don't let them turn it into an auction, John," he said. "Let's put in identical bids of £96,000, and then see what Jimmy says."

What Battersby did not know is that Bill had already been to Jimmy's apartment in Milan and had it confirmed that he wanted to play for Spurs. After Milan had announced that both clubs had

SCRAPBOOK MEMORIES: Bill gave me this interview just before swooping to buy Ralph Coates from Burnley for £192,000

bid the same, Battersby withdrew after Jimmy had made it clear he preferred the challenge of Tottenham rather than climbing the same mountains with Chelsea. Milan then decided they were not going to let him go for less than a world record £100,000, and in a tense meeting with the AC directors Bill told them: "You are turning this into a scene from Merchant of Venice and want your pound of flesh!"

All the journalists who got to report the marathon negotiations formed a Jimmy Greaves Club, and we had a special tie manufactured by Dave Mackay's company, with Greavsie as our president. The fee was first reported at £100,000, and it was not until Bill got back to London with his capture that it was officially confirmed at £99,999. Denis Law became the first £100,000 British footballer nine months later, when he joined Manchester City from Torino for £115,000

Bill, quite frugal with his own cash, bought boldly yet wiseley and always did his best to unload a player to bring down the price. It was Greavsie who went to West Ham as £54,000 makeweight in the deal that brought Martin Peters to the Lane, and Frank Saul was valued at £45,000 in the Martin Chivers move from Southampton for £125,000.

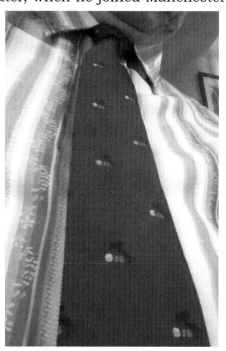

But for all his success in the transfer market, there was one who got away. Bill was desperate to sign Bobby Moore from West Ham and would have got him if England had not won the World Cup in 1966, with Mooro as the proud captain.

Listen in to this conversation I recorded between Jimmy Greaves and his best pal Bobby, reproduced here from

The Jimmy Greaves Club tie, still round my neck 53 years after his transfer to Tottenham. It has a football at the foot of a map of Italy and the initials JG. There were just two dozen made by Dave Mackay's company and we gave one to Bill Nick

my book *Bobby Moore, The Master* (all profits to the Bobby Moore Cancer Fund). I got them together for a reunion just a few months before we lost the irreplaceable Bobby to cancer:

JG: What a jammy git you were, Mooro, to last 90 matches as England captain. I did my best to cost you the job.

BM: Alf was often on the point of giving me the chop after incidents involving you, James. He went ballistic in New York in 1964 after you'd talked me into breaking a curfew to sneak away from the team hotel to see Ella Fitzgerald singing at Madison Square Garden.

JG: Dear old Alf. When we told him we'd been to see Ella he thought it was an elephant at the circus. All he knew about was football and westerns.

BM: Yeah, he loved his westerns. Remember when we were in East Germany and Alf found out there was a western showing with subtitles? He rounded us up and we all went off to the cinema. The film was dubbed in German, and as the subtitles started crawling along the bottom of the screen they were in Polish!

JG: We pissed ourselves. Alf loved us to do things together, to go round as a team as if tied by a rope.

BM: You were too much of an individualist for him, Jim. Don't forget that we were together on the best day of my life and the worst of yours.

JG: Knew you'd bring that up. We were room sharing in the Hendon Hall hotel during the 1966 World Cup. It was weird when we woke up on on the morning of the final because you KNEW you were going to captain the side and I GUESSED I wouldn't be playing. Alf had not said a dicky bird to me, but I sensed I'd been given the elbow.

BM: What could Alf do, Jim? You'd been injured for the quarter and semi-final and the team had been magnificent in both games. If there had been substitutes then you would have got on, and Geoff probably wouldn't have got his hat-trick.

JG: That's all blood under the bridge, Mooro. I always knew we would win the World Cup but, to be honest, I never envisaged that I would be a spectator. I wonder if people realise how close you came to not playing in the finals?

BM: Oh, you mean the West Ham contract business. I was virtually blackmailed into signing a new contract with the club just before the first match against Uruguay. Ron Greenwood came to the hotel with all the papers, and it was made clear to me that as I was out of contract with West Ham I would not, under Fifa rules, be eligible to play for England. I had been hanging out for a hoped-for move to join you at Tottenham, but West Ham kept copping a deaf ear to their approaches. So I put my name to the contract and came off the West Ham transfer list. I wasn't being greedy. I just knew I was getting paid half of what many of the players at other clubs were earning.

JG: You'd have loved it at Spurs. Bill Nicholson never made a secret of his admiration for your fooballing talent, and if you'd joined us in those mid-60s I reckon we could have got the League title to go with the FA Cup we won in '67.

BM: Don't rub it in, Jimbo. I was always a fan of that Tottenham team's style of play under Bill Nick. I got several pulls on the old hush-hush including from you that Bill wanted me, but West Ham would not budge. No disrespect to West Ham, but the overall strength of the Spurs squad was far superior back then to what we had at Upton Park.

Bill Nick confirmed after he had given up managing that Bobby was the player he had most wanted in the mid-60s. "He and Mike England would have been perfect partners," he told me, "but the moment England won the World Cup I knew there was no chance West Ham would let him go. They made him one of the highest paid players in the country, and he was worth every penny. He was a fantastic reader of the game, possibly as good as England has ever produced."

Something that always intrigued me with Bill is that we rarely saw him take a touchline seat. He much preferred to sit in the main stand at the Lane just behind the directors and immediately in front of the Press Box. We used to get a close up of the stress he went through during matches, but he always managed to control his emotions while making notes, and he was totally lost in a cocoon of concentration. He saw the game differently to we mere mortals. While we would be watching the man on the ball, his eyes would be on other parts of the pitch as he assessed what his players were doing off the ball.

It is interesting to see how the modern manager prefers a touchline base, whereas Nick, along with most of the outstanding managers from my reporting days – Sir Matt Busby, Stan Cullis, Shanks and Ron Greenwood – chose to watch from a seat in the stand. Each of them reckoned they got an enhanced overview and were able to make more complete tactical evaluations.

Bill Nick told me while still in charge at the Lane: "I dislike watching it from pitch level. You get a distorted view, and it's pointless shouting out instructions to the players because they can't hear you properly and it just leads to confusion. From the stand you get a complete view of the pitch and are better able to assess the team and individual performances. I have Eddie Baily sitting pitch side, and he makes enough noise for both of us!"

It was a painful and edifying experience to sit behind Stan Cullis, whose seat at Molineux – like Bill Nick's – was immediately in front of the Press Box. And like Nick, he kicked every ball and the wooden partition in front of him used to take a battering.

I once asked him if he wore out his shoes. He looked at me blankly, because he had no idea that he was kicking the furniture. Stan used to get so intensely involved in every match that he once drove off home alone after a game, forgetting he had taken his wife. Bill was equally intense but hid his fury when things were going wrong. He saved it for the dressing-room, and he was almost in the Alex Ferguson class for giving the hair-drying treatment.

But we never got to write about it. He was from the old school who believed what happened in the dressing-room stayed in the dressing-room. Steve Perryman summed it up: "He could really rip into you after a match, but when you analysed what he was saying he was nearly always right and you were a better player for it. One of the best coaches ever."

Chapter Ten
European
Travails

DURING my Fleet Street career I travelled thousands of miles with Bill, both on the Tottenham campaigns in Europe and as a member of the Press gang following the fortunes of the England Under-23 team that he used to manage on their summer tours. Every trip has special memories for me as I bask in the last of the summer wine, and to give this Bill Nicholson Revisited journey a different twist I have excavated three contrasting Tales of the Unexpected that provided Nick with a mixture of amusement, bemusement and not a little embarrassment.

First, we go back to the England Under-23 summer tour of 1967 that coincided with the Six-day War, and at the height of hostilities the squad was briefly stranded in Bulgaria. Bill Nick was in charge of 16 players, trainer Wilf McGuinness, six doddery members of the FA blazered brigade, and – stringing along – seven of Fleet Street's finest football writers. I would say that. I was one of them.

Along with Bill, the central character in this story is Peter Corrigan, a recently retired columnist on the *Independent on Sunday* and former sports editor of the *Observer* and certainly one of the finest and funniest journalists of my generation. At that time in 1967 Peter was reporting for the broadsheet *Sun* before it morphed into the soaraway tabloid toy of Murdoch.

As the war reached its peak, it suddenly became impossible to make telephone or telex contact with our London offices. I was earning my daily bread at the time with the *Express,* and along with my colleagues I sat fretting and frustrated in the team's hotel headquarters in Sofia as the edition deadlines approached and disappeared into the distance.

In those non-STD, pre-internet days you had to order your telephone calls through the hotel switchboard, and we were informed that all lines were down. You have to remember the mood at the time. There was wild rumour of Russia getting involved and nuclear weapons being used as Israeli tanks and jet fighters destroyed the combined forces of Egypt, Jordan and Syria. We agreed among us that if anybody should be lucky enough to get through, we would put over a shared story that could be distributed at the London end.

Bill Nick was aware of our communication problems because he too was unable to make contact with the UK, and was wondering if the plug should be pulled on the tour when war was waging not too far south of us and with fears that it could easily spread.

After two days of total silence, it was Peter Corrigan who suddenly got the desperately awaited call and found himself being put through to the *Sun* sports desk from the lobby of the hotel.

It was an appalling line and he was reduced to screaming "Peter Corrigan" into the mouthpiece in a bid to make himself heard at the other end.

Bill Nick joined the rest of us gathered around him, willing him to keep the precious line open. We couldn't believe it when he suddenly threw down the receiver without having dictated a word.

On the other end of the line had been a veteran sub-editor with a pronounced King George VI-style stutter. Peter, tearing out what little hair he had left, looked at us wild-eyed and said: "I've just been told that P-P-Peter C-C-Corrigan is in B-B-Bulgaria, and then he put the phone down and cut me off."

I seem to remember saying something like f-f-f-fancy that. Or words to that effect.

It was Bill who was first to see the funny side of it, and as he told the FA officials what had happened he could hardly talk for laughing, his 'dour Yorkshireman' image under threat.

Later in that same year of 1967 Tottenham made their return to European football, challenging for the Cup Winners' Cup they had won on an historical and hysterical night in Rotterdam in 1963. Their first match back in Europe was a difficult away tie against Yugoslavian cup holders Hajduk Split, a club with a reputation for crowd disturbances that had earned their supporters the nickname 'The Pirates.'

A born worrier, Bill was deeply concerned about the game and continually lectured the players about how brutal the Hajduk players could be and that on no account should they retaliate. "Don't worry," said comedian Cyril Knowles, "I'll get my retaliation in first."

Wound up to expect a hostile reception, you can imagine the embarrassed surprise of the Tottenham players when each of them was presented with a huge bouquet of flowers as they ran on to the pitch. Knowlesie led the way in throwing the flowers to the fans over the barbed-wired fence that was keeping the spectators at bay. Nice one, Cyril.

Goals from the two Jimmys – Robertson and Greaves – gave Spurs a comfortable 2-0 victory and the Hajduck fans turned on their own side, and burned club banners and threw the bouquets of flowers back on to the pitch, but this time they had been turned into flaming torches.

I had a huge laugh when looking up my scrapbook report on this match to find the headline: "GAY GREAVES MAKES THEM HOT SPURS.'

This was before 'gay' took on new meaning, and I've enjoyed bringing it to Greavsie's notice. It will amuse his four grown kids and small army of grandchildren to see the description.

Split (in Croatia, no longer Yugoslavia) is a picturesque town that nestles on the eastern shores of the Adriatic against the backdrop of the Dalmatian mountains, a miniature Monte Carlo dotted with casinos. All the major hotels have entertainment facilities and on the eve of the match we press reporters discovered something quite mind-blowing in a nightclub in our hotel, where Bill and the players were also staying. The highlight was an erotic dance by a stripper with an 80-inch bust. Yes, 80-inch. What she

Gay Greaves makes them hot Spurs

CALL IT FLOWER POWER

HOW to keep Soccer fans happy? Toss 'em a few flowers.

That's what Cyril Knowles and the Spurs team did before the start of their match with Hajduk.

But 90 minutes and two goals later the fans replied with rockets and fireworks.

From NORMAN GILLER

SPLIT (Yugoslavia), Wednesday.

Hajduk 0 Tottenham 2

European Cup-Winners' Cup — first round, first leg.

TOTTENHAM came marching back into European Soccer combat today in a blaze of glory.

Angry Yugoslav fans fired flaming rockets on to the pitch and burned club banners as Spurs efficiently mastered the overrated menace of Hajduk.

These notoriously hostile supporters—nicknamed the Pirates—turned on their own team after Spurs had plundered two goals from a cupboard of deep defence.

They jeered at every Hajduk player, and then fired rockets and flares from their terrace positions behind spiked bars and barbed wire.

Ripping

The Spurs goal was hidden for the last two minutes by a thick screen of smoke. It had been that way for the previous 88 minutes behind a cleverly organised eight-man defence that cruelly squeezed the spark and spirit out of the Spurs attack.

Spurs placed caution before confidence after going into a 4th-minute lead.

Jimmy Robertson got a pass from Jimmy Greaves and scored from close after Frank Saul had ripped the Hajduk defence apart with a thrust-and-dart run.

Greaves and Saul then left to concentrate on defensive duties, going to the attack only in rare moments.

SCRAPBOOK MEMORIES: A headline that shows how the meaning of words change over time. This was my 1967 match report for the Daily Express on Tottenham's winning match in Split in what was then Yugoslavia. That's Cyril Knowles throwing his bouquet to the Hajduk fans. At the end of the match the bouquet was thrown back as a flaming torch!

did with a length of knotted rope defied belief.

Bill was so buoyed by Tottenham's excellent victory that after the match he allowed our press gang to talk him into joining us in the nightclub for an assessment of the extraordinary striptease, on the understanding that nobody reported it.

Forty-six years later I am telling the story to reveal the human side of Bill Nicholson, without causing him any embarrassment with Darkie. He and his assistant Eddie Baily watched the strip act wide eyed, and Bill's verdict had us in fits. He said: "I think she could do a better job in the middle of our defence than Mike England! She would be able to chest the ball down."

Move the clock forward four years and Tottenham were back in Europe competing for the Uefa Cup that had taken over from the Inter-City Fairs Cup. We flew to Bucharest for a second leg tie against Rapid, who had gone down to a 3-0 defeat at White Hart Lane.

Hunter Davies, renowned author of the classic *The Glory Game*, was among the travelling party with his fly-on-the-wall eyes and given the freedom of the dressing-room by the usually almost secretive Nicholson. We daily newspapermen were green with envy, but knew the story of the club was in good hands with this master of observation.

The game went down in the Tottenham hall of shame as the Battle of Bucharest, and Hunter described in *The Glory Game* how I had reported in the *Express* that 'Spurs were hacked and kicked about like rag dolls.'

Bill Nick went on record with the view that Rapid were the dirtiest side he had seen in more than thirty years in football.

The dressing-room at the end of the match, won 2-0 by Spurs, was like a casualty clearing station, with six Spurs players nursing injuries caused by tackles that belonged in the house of horrors rather than on a football pitch.

I noticed that throughout the game assistant manager Eddie Baily had been bawling at Martin Chivers from the touchline bench, calling him every name to which he could put his merciless

Cockney tongue. You could not help but hear the insults being aimed at the Ambling Alp of Spurs because the huge stadium was barely a third full. Big Chiv had finally silenced Baily by scoring a superb goal, and you did not have to be a lip reader to know that Martin responded by shouting obscenities at his nemesis.

We flew straight back to London after the match, and I took careful note that Baily and Chivers completely ignored each other at the airport and on the flight. Later that week I saw Bill Nick privately and told him I was thinking of writing a story about the obvious enmity between his right hand man Eddie and his most productive forward, Martin.

Bill looked as pained as if I was telling him I was putting down his pet dog.

"I can't tell you what and what not to write," he said, "but let me just say that you'll not be doing me any favours. Off the record, we're having problems with Martin. He is a strong-minded young man who thinks he knows it all. His attitude drives Eddie bananas, but you know Eddie – he often shouts things in the heat of a match that he doesn't really mean. I'm trying to make the peace between them, and any story about them will only make matters worse."

Thank goodness I was helped off the hook by a breaking story that Arsenal were bidding £200,000 for Everton's Alan Ball, and I was able to follow Bill's request not to write about the simmering war between Baily and Chivers.

More than thirty years later I returned to the subject, this time when interviewing Eddie Baily following the passing of Bill Nick. I had known Eddie well from his days at Orient, a club that was on my local paper beat. He was in the winding down period of his playing career and he hardly used to move outside the centre-circle, but he had lost none of the precision of his passing and he continually found team-mates with balls delivered with stunning accuracy.

Eddie was from my East London manor, a loud, humorous, opinionated man who could have been the model for Alf Garnett but more likable. He was stockily built, with powerful thighs and footballer's legs so bowed that you could have driven a pig through them without him knowing. He seemed never to be able to forget that he served his country with distinction in the Second World War with the Royal Scots Fusiliers and was always using wartime phrases. He invariably sent the team out on to the field with the instruction: "Fix bayonets, chaps, time to go over the top."

In the early days of the war he was an amateur with Spurs. While fighting abroad it was reported to Tottenham that he had been killed in action, and his name was removed from their books. On his demob he signed with Chelsea, but once the mistake had been pointed out he was allowed to rejoin his first-choice club Tottenham in February 1946. It is difficult to imagine Arthur Rowe's Push and Run tactics would have been so successful without the Baily passes to make the team tick.

He was reunited with Bill Nicholson as coach at Tottenham in 1963 after Bill's assistant, Harry Evans, had been cruelly lost to cancer at the age of 43. Harry was father-in-law to John White, so the family was ripped apart by two appalling tragedies in just a couple of years.

Baily was the perfect foil and balance to the quieter, more thoughtful and constructive Nicholson. The 'bad cop' to the 'good cop.' Eddie could hardly get a sentence out without decorating it with swear words, while Bill rarely turned to obscenities to make his point. But there were players that brought even Bill to four-letter-word territory, and chief among them was Martin Chivers, a hugely gifted player who was for a couple of seasons one of the greatest centre-forwards in the world after recovering from a serious knee injury that threatened his career.

I told Eddie how Bill had asked me not to write about his dispute with Chivers. "I wish you had written it," he said. "Martin needed bringing down a peg or two. If he'd been a bar of chocolate he would have eaten himself. He had everything going for him, built like a Greek god but too often playing like a big Jesse. I could never forgive him for his disrespect to Bill, and more than once I said we should have got rid of him. He caused a bad atmosphere in the dressing-room with his attitude. When we left the club in 1974 Bill had been negotiating to swap him with Stan Bowles at Queen's Park Rangers. Bowles in a Spurs shirt would have been interesting."

I made a stand for Chivers. "Be fair, Eddie," I said, "there were a couple of seasons when he was the best centre-forward in the country."

"In the country maybe, but not the town," joked Eddie, who rarely missed a chance to try to show why during his playing days he was nicknamed the Cheeky Chappie after music hall comedian Max Miller.

He added seriously: "I remember you stupidly writing that he was the greatest England centre-forward of all time. That went right to his head and he started to believe his own publicity. What an insult to the likes of Tommy Lawton, Nat Lofthouse, Dixie Dean, Bobby Smith and Jackie Milburn. He was not fit to clean the boots of my old mucker in the Push and Run side, Len Duquemin."

The inevitable war metaphor followed. "I would not have wanted to have Chivers alongside me in a trench."

I reminded Eddie of the two classic Chivers goals at Wolves that virtually won the Uefa Cup for Spurs, and how he had kowtowed to him in the dressing-room afterwards.

"He was fantastic that night," he conceded, "but with all that ability he should have done it week in and week out. But he'd just disappear from matches and seemed not to care. I never knew a more aggravating footballer. He had it all but too often did eff all."

I waited for the steam to stop coming out of Eddie's ears, and then asked for his assessment of Bill Nick as a manager.

"He was one of the greatest managers there has ever been," he said. "Matt Busby, Bill Shankly, Arthur Rowe, Stan Cullis, Alf and Bill, they were the best of my time. The only thing he was not good at was delegation. He tried to do everything and worked himself into the ground for the club. And how did they reward him? Let him go with a pathetic pay-off that players today can

SCRAPBOOK MEMORIES: This was my praising-to-the-hilt article on Martin Chivers that had Spurs coach Eddie Baily hopping mad. He thought I had gone way over the top in my assessment of Big Chiv as one of the greatest England centre-forwards of all time. Regardless of what Eddie thought, I stand by my view that for a couple of seasons Martin was up there with the legends of the game like Tommy Lawton and Nat Lofthouse.

earn in a day. To rub it in they delayed the cheques to me and Bill for so long we both had to sign on the dole. How humiliating."

The swearwords that peppered Eddie's outburst have been censored.

I reminded Eddie that when he was playing he tried to maximize his earnings, There was, for example, an advertisement in which he endorsed Craven "A" cigarettes – "they offer smooth clean smoking". The ad quoted Baily as saying: "You'd be surprised how dry your mouth feels after a big match. That's why I stay with Craven "A". Whenever I light one up, the flavour of the tobacco comes through mellow and satisfying, just the way I want it. I couldn't afford to smoke a cigarette that irritated my throat."

Eddie was not in the least bit embarrassed when I pointed out the advertisement. "You have to remember," he said, "that when I endorsed those fags nobody knew how they caused cancer, and I was earning just fifteen quid a week. I owed it to my family to get every penny I could. That was one of the things that got me angry with Bill. He did his job for peanuts, which meant none of his staff could earn decent money either. We had a short fall out when we left Spurs. I felt I deserved a crack at managing the club, but Bill wouldn't put my name forward. He said with that no-nonsense honesty of his the Board would not want me, and he pushed for Danny instead. I got the right hump over that. But our friendship was strong enough to get us over that little squabble. I loved the bloke really, you know. The most honest man I ever met. Too honest for his own good."

I couldn't resist asking Eddie a loaded Spurs question: "How would the Push and Run side have got on against the Double team?"

"I'm biased because I played for the Push and Run team," he said. "I am tempted to say we would have won by a couple of goals, but let's settle for a score draw."

Eddie passed on six years after his pal Bill Nick. Both reached 85. Both unforgettable. Both with the spirit of Spurs deep in their soul. Both hugely missed.

Chapter Eleven
It Takes Two to Tango

COMEDIAN Eric Morecambe knew before most people that Spurs were about to pull off the most sensational transfer coup in British football history in the summer of 1978, and it was our hero Bill Nicholson who made it all happen. Please be patient while I explain. Or – as Eric would have said – while I try to get the words down, not necessarily in the right order.

For several years I had the privilege and pleasure of working with Eric on regular newspaper columns for the *Daily Express* and the magazine *Titbits*, which was a weekly, all-topics chat publication and nothing to do with a woman's anatomy. Eric's share of the fees used to be paid to Luton Town Football Club, where he was the jester director who got the Hatters more publicity than they'd had before or since.

The manager at Luton for much of Eric's time on the board was a charismatic character called Harry Haslam, who was rarely seen without a smile on his face as he lived up to his nickname 'Happy Harry.' Whenever I used to be in the company of Eric and Harry at Luton's Kenilworth Road ground it was a toss up who got more laughs. Yes, Harry was *that* funny.

Now to get to the point. In 1978 Harry took over at Sheffield United but still kept in close contact with the Harpenden-based comedian. I was discussing our column with Eric when he said: "Shall we write about the two Argentines who are going to play in England? You know, lines like it takes two to tango but it will be more of a knees up when Bites Yer Legs gets stuck into them."

Eric often had me speechless with laughter, but this time I was lost for words because of the unusual facts he was offering.. "What two Argentines?" I asked. "Is this a joke?"

Morecambe and Unwise: I am getting the facts from Eric, not necessarily in the right order circa 1978. I have enough hair for both of us, and you can't see the join. Give me sunshine ...

He then explained how Harry had told him that his Argentine coach (Oscar Arce) had wanted him to buy two members of the squad who had just won the World Cup in Buenos Aires. Sheffield United could not afford them and so Harry had tipped off two of his closest friends in the game, Bill Nicholson at Tottenham and Terry Neill at Arsenal.

The names of the two players who were desperate to play in England: Osvaldo Ardiles and Ricardo Villa.

I immediately telephoned Bill Nick, who had been quite properly reinstalled at Tottenham by manager Keith Burkinshaw, with the backing of new chairman Irving Scholar after a brief spell as a fish out of water at West Ham. He was now employed at his beloved Lane as chief scout, and was enjoying the role of helping plot the team's future without the crushing pressure of being the manager. Keith, one of the nicest men you could wish to meet, always kept him in the loop and often quietly asked his advice. There was never a hint of interference from Bill, only sincere interest.

As readers of this book will testify, I can waffle for England, but I came straight to the point.

"Bill, what d'you know of Osvaldo Ardiles and Ricardo Villa?"

There was a silence on the phone that could have been measured in fathoms. "What do YOU know?" he finally asked.

I told him about my conversation with Eric.

"Well Eric is bang on the ball," he said. "Even as I speak Keith is in Argentina hopefully wrapping up the deal. I passed on Harry's tip to Keith and the directors and they are as excited as me about the possibility of signing them. We know Arsenal are interested but thanks to Harry we've got a head start."

Driven by the hungry writer inside me, I contacted powerhouse *Sun* sports editor Frank Nicklin with the tip. "Too late, old son," he said. "It's just come over the wires from Buenos Aires. Burkinshaw has signed them both. We're leading the front and back pages on it in the morning. It's the soccer story of the century. Spurs Beat Arsenal In Argie Bargie."

That was how Frank talked, in *Sun* headlines.

Sure enough Ardiles and Villa arrived at the Lane at the start of what was a revolution in English football. Both were wonderful ambassadors for football, for Tottenham and for their country, and Villa's magical solo goal in the 1981 FA Cup final replay against Manchester City has been cemented into Spurs folklore.

But as I write in 2013 I wonder what Bill Nick would make of it all, now that you cannot move in football's village for foreign owners, footballers, managers and coaches.

And what would he make of the salaries? The fact that a fairly average player can now command a £100,000 a week wage would have blown Bill's mind. He earned less in his entire career.

The one major criticism that his players had was that he was miserly with the club's money when it came to negotiating new contracts, but Bill was from the school that admired Dickens and his Mr. Micawber logic: "Annual income twenty pounds, annual expenditure nineteen [pounds] nineteen [shillings] and six [pence], result happiness. Annual income twenty pounds, annual expenditure twenty pounds ought and six, result misery."

Bill was almost Corinthian in his outlook, and would willingly have played the game for nothing. When his players were continually moaning in confidence to me about the fact they felt underpaid, I used to think back to the first interview I had with Bill in 1958: "If you can't live on £20 a week, then there's something wrong with your housekeeping."

Lane Legend Cliff Jones recalled: "Bill was a terrier when you tried to negotiate with him. The year we won the Cup Winners' Cup I was on £65 a week and got a £100 bonus for that historic victory. I went to see Bill in his office and said I deserved a pay rise because the press were saying I was the best winger in Europe. Bill said, 'That's a matter of opinion and it's not mine' ... and he told me to shut the door on the way out." But I still rate him the greatest manager of them all. He put the club first at all times."

During his exceptional managing career, Bill brought many young British footballers through the ranks. I am thinking of the

SCRAPBOOK MEMORIES: Two of Bill's favourite footballers (and mine) are featured here, Steve Perryman in his debut season and the sophisticated Scottish artist Alan Gilzean

likes of Steve Perryman, Philip Beal, Joe Kinnear, John Pratt, Jimmy Pearce, Jimmy Neighbour, Eddie Clayton, Frank Saul and Glenn Hoddle. Today, overseas players are quickly brought in to take the positions young British players had been dreaming of filling. As good as they are to watch, the invasion of foreign players leaves me feeling uncomfortable. What would that great traditionalist Bill Nick have thought? Look what you started, Bill!

As lovely Eric Morecambe would say, "Now there's a novelty!"

In the winter of 1983 I got myself and a publisher excited about a book called BILL NICHOLSON: MY WINNING SPURS

I spent a day putting together an in-depth synopsis, focusing on all the players Bill had signed in the days when he continually broke the British transfer record to bring to the Lane the likes of Dave Mackay, John White, Jimmy Greaves, Alan Gilzean,Mike England, Martin Chivers, Martin Peters, and Ralph Coates. My idea was to get Bill talking in depth about every deal, and explaining his thinking behind putting together the pieces of each of his great teams

I had the publisher (Roddy Bloomfield, the legendary driving force at Hodder & Stoughton), I had the format, now all I had to do was to convince Bill Nick to climb aboard. I knew I could not persuade him with money because Bill had famously never been motivated by profit, so I came up with the idea to donate the royalties to a Tottenham schools football project.

I went to Bill with my grand idea and was crushed when he told me that he had already signed a contract to write his autobiography, with my old Fleet Street colleagues Brian Scovell and Harry Harris as his ghostwriters.

They did a splendid job with their 1984 book published by Macmillan: *Glory Glory My Life with Spurs*, and I greatly recommend it for all those who want to know everything about Bill Nick's life and times.

But, of course, *My Winning Spurs* would have been much better. It was the best book what I never wrote.

Eric Morecambe: "The boy's a fool!"

Chapter Twelve
At home with Bill

IT was a double-decker red bus that had taken me to my first meeting with Bill Nicholson in 1958, now here I was 43 years later in my Spurs-blue 4.2 Jaguar driving to see The Master for what was to prove the last face-to-face interview. It was the week before the testimonial Tottenham were belatedly giving him at White Hart Lane and I was sounding him out for a proposed appearance on a television programme I had devised.

This was a series called *Who's the Greatest?*, and we were planning to feature Jimmy Greaves against Kenny Dalglish in a revival of the show that had run on ITV in the 1980s. I wanted to know whether Bill would be prepared to appear as a witness for Greavsie, while also craftily picking his brains for more treasured recollections about all things Spurs.

I prepared to park my flash car outside his modest but welcoming 71 Creighton Road N.17. home, a small, unpretentious house once owned by Spurs and rented to him until he became sole owner in the 1960s "for a couple of thousand pounds." It was close enough to the Lane that on match days you could hear the roar of the crowd.

Bill opened his front door as I pulled up, leaning heavily on a stick that was his one concession to galloping old age. "I remember you when you couldn't afford a bike," was his opening shot, immediately reviving memories of the banter we always used to share when I was doing my bread-and-butter job of football reporting.

"You can't park there," he said. "You'll get a ticket. Drive round the back where you'll find our garage in a block. I won't charge you for taking our space. First right and then an immediate left."

Bill Nick, looking all of his 82 years, was still showing the way; still giving directions. Keep it simple. Give it and go. When not in possession get in position

The delightful Darkie demanded I have a cup of tea and then disappeared to the local shops – walking, I noticed, rather than cycling – and leaving her beloved Bill and I to our rose-coloured recollections; or perhaps that should be blue and white.

The Nicholsons, approaching their Diamond Wedding, had one of those end-of-terrace houses that hug you, nothing whatsoever ostentatious about it but warm, welcoming and filled with friendliness. Their snug lounge led into an extension that was decorated with family photographs, mostly of daughters Linda and Jean and much-loved grandchildren. Just a framed photo of Bill proudly showing off his OBE in the Buckingham Palace forecourt gave any hint that this was the home of a hero. This was the comfortable sanctuary to which Bill used to escape after all those triumphs in vast stadiums filled with cheering, chanting fans. What a contrast.

"Still tending your allotment?" I asked from my seat on the sofa, with him relaxed opposite me in his favourite, well-worn armchair, wearing a cardigan and Marks and Spencer slippers. His hair was still military-short but the once gingery, then steel grey had surrendered to a whiteness that would have matched a Spurs shirt.

"No, the old joints are not up to it now," he said. "But the neighbours keep it tidy and under control. The blackberry bush I planted is still there and giving us fruit."

Just a few months earlier during the welter of litigation that tarnished the club in what were uncertain times there had been a tense exchange in the High Court. Former chairman Sir Alan Sugar, in his libel action against Associated Newspapers, denied vehemently the accusation by the newspaper's QC that, "On one occasion you were introduced to Bill Nicholson and were heard to say, 'Who is that old git?'"

When it was reported I remember all supporters with Spurs in their soul were outraged. This was like not knowing who lived at Buckingham Palace.

"What did you think of that?" I asked Bill, convinced he would give me one of his famous blanks.

"I thought it was hilarious," he said, unexpectedly. "I could

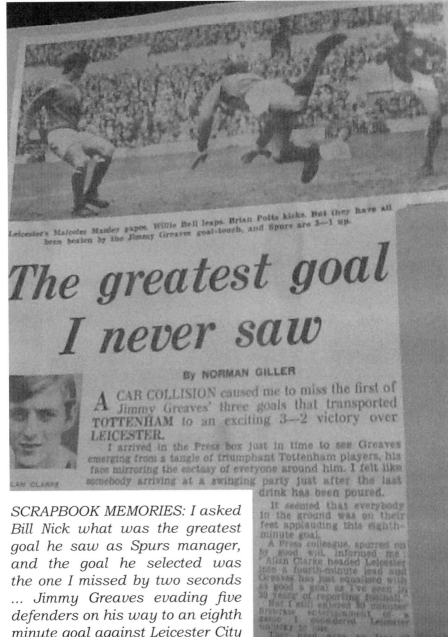

Leicester's Malcolm Manley gapes. Willie Bell leaps. Brian Potts kicks. But they have all been beaten by the Jimmy Greaves goal-touch, and Spurs are 3—1 up.

The greatest goal
I never saw

By NORMAN GILLER

A CAR COLLISION caused me to miss the first of Jimmy Greaves' three goals that transported TOTTENHAM to an exciting 3—2 victory over LEICESTER.

I arrived in the Press box just in time to see Greaves emerging from a tangle of triumphant Tottenham players, his face mirroring the ecstasy of everyone around him. I felt like somebody arriving at a swinging party just after the last drink has been poured.

It seemed that everybody in the ground was on their feet applauding this eighth-minute goal.

A Press colleague, spurred on by good will, informed me: "Allan Clarke headed Leicester into a fourth-minute lead and Greaves has just equalised with as good a goal as I've seen in 30 years of reporting football."

Not that I still enjoyed 90 minutes entertainment ... at least a game I considered Leicester unlucky to lose.

SCRAPBOOK MEMORIES: I asked Bill Nick what was the greatest goal he saw as Spurs manager, and the goal he selected was the one I missed by two seconds ... Jimmy Greaves evading five defenders on his way to an eighth minute goal against Leicester City in 1968. Doh!

have said exactly the same thing about Sugar!"

When I tried to press Bill on the subject of boardroom battles and bungs, he waved a finger at me like an admonishing headmaster. "How long have we known each other?"

"More than 40 years," I said.

"And when have you ever known me get involved in politics? It is just not my scene. All I was ever interested in was the football. Keith Burkinshaw shared my views on that and it's why he quit the club. He was a first-class manager and I thought it was bonkers when the club let him go. The only time I got into politics was when I tried to get Danny Blanchflower appointed as my successor as manager, and all that got me was the embarrassment of having the Board completely ignore my advice."

I could sense Bill was uncomfortable talking club matters, perhaps conscious that he was still Tottenham's honorary President, so I changed the subject.

"We are reviving a TV series I dreamt up in the 1980s called Who's the Greatest?" I explained, "and one of our first shows will feature celebrities and experts arguing the case for Jimmy Greaves against Kenny Dalglish."

"Hasn't that already been on?"

"That was Greaves against Ian Rush. We had a jury of twelve people and they voted eight-four in Jimmy's favour."

It set Bill off on the road down memory lane. "Should have been twelve-nought! Jimmy was the greatest scorer of them all. I've never seen a player touch him for putting the vital finishing touch. While others were still thinking about what to do, whoosh, he would just get on and do it. He would have the ball into the net in the blinking of an eye and then amble back to the centre-circle as casually as if he'd just swatted a fly. A genius."

Bill's mind was now filled with action replays of golden goals from the boots of our mutually favourite footballer, Greavsie. Not the rotund, funny one on the telly. This, the 10st 8lbs lightning-quick, darting, dribbling, twisting, turning and passing the ball into the net Jimmy Greaves, the Artful Dodger penalty area pickpocket who snaffled more memorable goals than many of us have had hot baths.

"He never gave me a spot of trouble. you know," Bill continued, now thinking aloud rather than talking direct to me. I need not have been there. He was wandering around a precious past, and did not need any prompting or interruption. "Even when it came time for us to part company he knew in his heart he'd lost his appetite for the game. People who didn't know what they were talking about sometimes described him as a bit of a faint-heart, but in all the years I watched him I never ever saw him shirk a tackle. And I'll tell you what, there were at least ten goals that should have been added to his career total. Time and again he would be flagged off-side simply because his movement was too quick for the eye of the linesman.

"The hardest of all to take was in the 1962 European Cup semi-final against Benfica here (Bill waved a gnarled hand at the wall in the direction of nearby White Hart Lane) when he scored a perfectly good goal that was ruled off-side. That broke all our hearts. We might have beaten Jock (Stein) and his great Celtic to become the first British team to win the European Cup.

"Jimmy had two great partnerships for us, first with Bobby Smith who provided lots of muscle in making openings for Jimmy, and then with Alan Gilzean, one of the most elegant forwards I've ever clapped eyes on. Greavsie and Gilly together were like poetry in motion. I was hoping for a third one when I put Jim together with Martin Chivers, but by then he was only giving half his attention to the game. He was quite the businessman off the pitch, and that took the edge off his appetite for football.

"But even with half his concentration he was still twice as good as any other goal-scoring forward. It hurt like hell the day I decided to let him go in part exchange for Martin Peters. But as a manager you often had to do things that hurt you inside but were necessary for the team and the club. Martin was another wonderfully gifted footballer, but completely different to Jim. Alf (Ramsey) described him as being ten years ahead of his time, and I knew exactly what he meant. He was an exceptional reader of the game, a bit like Danny and dear John White, and knew where to be before anybody else had spotted the gap.

"Nothing's changed. Ball's still round. The game is still all about positioning. If you're not in the right place, then you're not going to be able to do the right thing. Positioning, positioning, positioning. The three Ps. Now Jimmy always knew where to be to make the most of a goal-scoring opportunity. It came naturally to him. You couldn't teach it. Quite a few of his goals were tap-ins, and people said he was lucky. He made his own luck by being in the right place at the right time."

I reluctantly brought Bill out of his golden reminiscing. "Would you be prepared to come to the studio and say that on camera?" I asked

Bill looked at me as if I had just awoken him from a wonderful dream

"You know I hate appearing in front of TV cameras," he said. "Hated it when I was a manager, hate it now. I'm a football man not a song and dance man. Mind you, I got a lot of pleasure watching Jimmy on the Saint and Greavsie show. Why did they take that off? I thought it was a good thing to show football could laugh at itself."

My eyebrows reached for the sky. "That's rich coming from you, Bill. You were Mr Serious throughout your managerial career.. Sometimes Mr Bleeding Miserable."

"That's true," he admitted, with a chuckle. "I found it difficult to unwind. I could never understand how the likes of Tommy Docherty, Brian Clough and Malcolm Allison could sometimes act like clowns. I never had that sort of release. For me football was, still is, much more than just a game. It was my life."

"You and Tommy Doc were big rivals in the 60s. But you got the better of him in the one that really mattered, the 1967 FA Cup final."

Suddenly the years fell away from the octogenarian as he dipped back into his peak seasons. "I was really worried about that one because Chelsea had stuffed us good and proper at the Bridge, 3-0 and it could have been five," he recalled. "They were playing a sweeper system, with Marvin Hinton very efficient in the role. Alan Gilzean detested that method and was much less effective against it. I was really concerned. Then, during the week of the final, talkative Tommy gave an interview in which he said he was dropping the sweeper formation and playing orthodox. I was delighted to hear it, and we were able to beat them 2-1."

"Which was the most satisfying of your FA Cup final victories?"

Bill gazed into space, like a man trying to choose between sparkling diamonds sitting in his memory bank. "Obviously from an achievement point of view it has to be the 1961 final because it completed what people described as the 'impossible' double, but to be honest I felt flat at the end of it because we did not play anything like our best against a Leicester team playing above itself. They were virtually down to ten men because of injury, and it somehow made the game lop-sided. There was no rhythm or pattern, while most of that season we'd played some of the finest football I've ever seen from a club side. You could have set it to music, it was so rhythmical. But the final turned out to be a big anti-climax. We got the Double, yes, But I wanted us to do it in real style, more for our wonderful fans than for me.

"The following year Jimmy gave us a great start with a magnificent goal after just three minutes and we beat a very talented Burnley side 3-1. That was probably the most satisfying, because we played it the Spurs way. Quick, simple, beautiful football. Never complicate what is basically a simple game, and treat the ball with respect not as if it's your worst enemy and needs a good hard kicking. Caress it, play it with care, make every pass count, and when not in possession get into position."

I dragged Bill away from the mantra he had been preaching for more than 60 years. "If you had to pick one match from all those in which you were involved as manager which gets your vote as the most satisfying?"

Back to the bank vault, and this time he had little hesitation in replying. "It has to be the 5-1 victory over Atletico Madrid in the 1963 European Cup Winners' Cup final," he said firmly. "This made us the first British team ever to win a major European trophy. That's in the history books forever. A bit special. The amazing thing was we managed it without arguably our best player, Dave Mackay. That was little Terry Dyson's big night. He scored two storming goals. I remember that old rascal Bobby Smith saying to him in the dressing-room afterwards that he should retire because he would never top that performance. Terry played on for another six years!"

Bill chuckled to himself over that suddenly uncorked memory, and I stupidly ruined the mood by introducing a sombre topic.

"Eddie Baily told me he was disgusted with the pay-off he got from Spurs, and that you didn't get much more."

I had dropped winter's discontent into his glorious summer. Bill was clearly not keen to discuss the subject, particularly with his testimonial match just a few days away. "Let's just say it was more a tin than a golden handshake," he said. "I only had myself to blame. I never had a contract with the club. I never wanted to put them in a position where if they wanted to get rid of me they couldn't because of a piece of paper. What hurt was having to sign on the dole. It should never have come to that. Eddie was bitter for a long time, and we fell out over it. We've since patched it up and when we get together we talk about the many good times we enjoyed rather than the unhappy finish."

With the insensitivity that made me so suitable to the journalistic profession, I continued with the negativity: "Martin Chivers gave you a lot of headaches in your last couple of seasons as manager."

"Yes, he became a real handful," Bill admitted, shaking his head as if to get rid of bad thoughts. "He and Eddie really disliked each other, which led to a heavy atmosphere. There were a couple of seasons when Martin was comfortably the outstanding centre-forward in the League, and it seemed to go to his head. He more than anybody put me in the mood to resign with his continual beefing about his wages, that and the terrible hooliganism that started to ruin so many games. To be honest, I was worn out by it all.

"Since he retired, Martin has gone out of his way to make amends by visiting me a lot, and he has apologised for his behaviour. He has developed into a really nice person, and we get on just fine. When Darkie meets him he makes a fuss of her, and she says, 'How on earth did a nice young man like that manage to upset you so much? You were always moaning about him, yet he strikes me as being a real charmer.' But Darkie did not have to put up with him constantly complaining about his wages and sulking when things didn't go his way."

SCRAPBOOK MEMORIES: This was a British record deal at the time, and Bill Nick was convinced he had found a great new playmate for Jimmy Greaves. But Martin was handicapped by an appalling knee injury, and by the time he recovered Greavsie had lost his appetite and was bound for West Ham. Today, that £125,000 would not pay Gareth Bale half his week's wages at Real Madrid. I can hear Greavsie: "It's a funny old game ..."

£125,000

CHIVERS

HAS NO

FEARS

By NORMAN GILLER

MARTIN CHIVERS yesterday became Britain's most expensive footballer when he signed for Spurs in a transfer that added up to £125,000.

But if Frank Saul, goal-scoring hero for Spurs in last year's Cup Final, had not agreed to join Southampton as a £45,000 part of the transfer, then the whole deal could have fallen through.

Spurs boss Bill Nicholson explained last night: " Southamp...

I was kicking myself for bruising our conversation by bringing in bad vibes from the past, and decided to put us back on smiling ground. "Of all the managers of your era, Bill, who did you get on with best of all?"

This was much more acceptable. "No question, it had to be Bill Shankly," he replied, his eyes twinkling at the thought of his old friend. "We used to talk regularly on the phone at least once a week. Bill was a very funny man, but deadly serious about football in something of a fanatical way. Once after Jimmy had scored one of his magical winning goals against Liverpool, he phoned me on the Monday and said, 'Bill, there's one thing wrong with that wee Greaves feller of yours. He wears the wrong colour shirt. He deserves to be in Liverpool red, playing for a proper team.' It's no coincidence that Bill and I both decided to get out at about the same time. We each felt that the game was not what it was.

"We would discuss all the football gossip, and put the world to rights. Darkie used to tease that we were like a couple of old women. Both Bill and I agreed that Brian Clough needed reining in. Bill used to say to me, 'When I talk to that man on the phone I'm never sure if he's drunk with arrogance or alcohol.'"

Bill peered into his teacup as if searching for a lost memory. "I don't think Brian ever forgave me for dropping him when I was manager of the England Under-23s," he confided. "It probably held back his promotion to the senior team, because I told England manager Walter Winterbottom that I considered him a bit of a lazy so-and-so who played more for himself than the team. I had to call it as I saw it."

And there it was. Bill Nicholson, in a sentence, "I had to call it as I saw it."

As honest as the day is long. He was the most refreshingly candid and trustworthy man I ever met in football.

He tossed in one surprise that took my breath away as I was preparing to leave. "I wonder how different my life would have been," he said, "if I had taken the offer to manage Sheffield Wednesday?"

"When was that?" I asked, wondering if he was pulling my leg.

"After the World Cup in 1958," he said. "Wednesday general

manager Eric Taylor sounded me out. He said he had been impressed by my coaching work with England during the World Cup finals in Sweden and wanted to know if I would be interested in taking over as team manager at Hillsborough. But I was happy coaching at Tottenham, and living here with our young family. Within a few weeks of being offered the job I was promoted manager at Spurs. Wednesday appointed Harry Catterick, and he turned them into our biggest rivals in that Double season. As your mate Greavsie would say, 'It's a funny old game.'"

I could not get my head round what Bill had told me. Manager of Sheffield Wednesday rather than Spurs? No, that was too much for my poor old brain to handle. Tottenham without Bill Nick? That was like the war without Churchill, English classics without Elgar, literature without Dickens. It was unthinkable.

Yes, I am exaggerating to make my point. Bill *was* Mr. Spurs.

Incidentally, I never did get him to appear in front of the cameras, but he will always remain on my memory screen.

Bill had a final word as we shook hands. "You know the hardest thing about managing?" he asked, chuckling. "It's that people who can't trap a bag of cement think they can do a better job."

My last view of Bill that memorable day I visited him at home was him leaning on his stick, waving me goodbye with a wide smile on a friendly face far removed from the 'dour Yorkshireman' description that accompanied so many of his interviews in his managing days. He was enjoying the last of the sumer wine, and it was vintage Tottenham.

Just for the record, my *Who's the Greatest* idea morphed into *Petrolheads*, a series I devised for BBC2. I could not see Bill appearing in that. The panel, headed by *Top Gear's* Richard Hammond, would have mocked him unmercifully for driving an unfashionable Vauxhall Cavalier.

Bill would not have cared less. After all, he had driven the best: a Rolls Royce of a football team called Tottenham Hotspur.

As I drove away from Creighton Road, the thought sat in my mind: Perhaps the people of Tottenham can put up a Spurs-blue plaque outside No 71: Bill Nicholson, The Master of White Hart Lane, lived here.

Chapter Thirteen
Nick's night
of Nostalgia

THERE was an extraordinary sight at Bill Nick's testimonial match at White Hart Lane on Wednesday August 8 2001. The old master came out on to the pitch to acknowledge an explosion of cheers from a ground full of worshippers, and we were astonished to see he was balanced on the supporting arm of his old nemesis, Martin Chivers.

For those of us who were close to Bill and all things Spurs in the 1970s this was the last pairing we ever expected to see. It just shows how time really can be a great healer. Big Chiv – now big affable Chiv – was looking after Bill like a caring son.

It was Martin who told Bill to leave his walking stick in the dressing-room. "You don't want your fans to see you needing that," he told him, and used his considerable strength to help him walk out on to his beloved White Hart Lane pitch for the last time to the sort of reception reserved for gods.

There was a near capacity crowd of 35,877 to see Spurs play Fiorentina in a pre-season friendly but, much more than that, they were there to pay homage to the man who for so many years represented the soul and the spirit of Spurs.

Bill was visibly moved by the warmth – the love – that showered down on him. He had never been demonstrative, an exhibitionist or a braggart; had never chased the cheers. Yet here was proof positive that the quiet man from Scarborough had won the hearts of an army of fans who appreciated and respected his lifetime's service to Tottenham and to football.

"This is one of the proudest nights of my life," Bill said through a boulder in his throat as the roar of the crowd almost deafened him. "I always told my players that the most important people were the supporters who paid their wages. Here they are proving it. I am overwhelmed."

143

Bill Nick happy at eighty, captured by artist Art Turner

The caring, considerate Chivers, holding the elderly and now frail Nicholson steady, told him: "You can feel the love, Bill. You've earned every one of these cheers."

The cynics among us could not believe that this was the same Martin Chivers who had battled with Bill on every front, from contracts to tactics, and had shown him scant respect.

"My differences with Bill and Eddie were greatly exaggerated and a lot of things were said in the heat of the moment," Chiv explained after steering the idolised former Spurs boss to his front row seat in the stands. "Bill knows how I feel about him, and how much I respect all he has done for this great club. He should be knighted for his services to football. Nobody has put more into the game than him. It's a pleasure for me to have him and Darkie as good friends."

Many eyes, including Bill's, were filled with tears as a parade of his old players lined up to pay tribute to him, including Mel Hopkins, Cliff Jones, Bobby Smith, Dave Mackay, Ron Henry, Tony Marchi, Les Allen, Pat Jennings, Martin Peters, Ralph Coates, John Pratt, Terry Naylor, the contrite Chivers and one of his last signings, Gary Mabbutt.

"The clock has turned back for me tonight," Bill said. "To see all my old players here is just wonderful. We had so many good times together, and throughout my managing career I tried to make it a family club ... and all the supporters were part of that family. I want to thank everybody a million times over for coming out for my special night. They have, as they say, made an old man very happy."

Once the shooting and the shouting was over (Spurs beat Fiorentina 3-0) I was delighted to be reunited with one of the great characters from Bill's Double-winning team, the one and only Bobby Smith. He was not in the greatest shape following a series of operations as his past caught up with him. During his career he continually played through the pain threshold with the help of cortisone injections, and he was hobbling more heavily than Bill. The price our heroes pay for their fame.

"One of the bravest footballers I ever knew," was Bill's sincere rating. "His feet were often so swollen he could hardly get his boots on, but he would insist on going out and playing. He was big hearted, could really thump the ball and had a lot more skill than people realised. He was the perfect target man and a master at laying off the ball and then getting into space for the return pass. Off the pitch he could be a bit of a rascal and I had to give him quite a few lectures, but he was good hearted and was always repentant. I was quite fond of him, for all our different way of living our lives. I could never understand gamblers like him and Alfie Stokes. Betting is such a mug's game."

Like Bill a Yorkshireman, Bobby could never be described as dour and we laughed over shared memories of a career that was a rollercoaster of highs and lows. He was a constant companion of controversy that often drove Bill Nick to hair-tearing despair.

We agreed on that testimonial night that I would get his incredible life story down on paper, with our mutual friend Terry Baker lined up as publisher. But – just like *Bill Nicholson's Winning Spurs* – it was a book that was never published

It was going to be called *Bobby Smith: Secrets of a Soccer Slave*. Everything was planned and I had collected and collated much of the material, which would have shocked the life out of today's pampered footballing millionaires.

But the secrets will go to the grave with Bobby, who lost his fight with cancer in 2010 before we had the chance to get into print.

The mighty Smith knew the best and worst of times. He was 28 before he earned more than £20 a week, and when joining Spurs from Chelsea in 1956, he was taking home just £17 a week.

In the 1960-61 season that he blasted Tottenham to the League championship and FA Cup double with 33 goals, the maximum wage was lifted. The following season – along with the rest of the double-winning players and newcomer Jimmy Greaves – he was paid a princely £65 a week.

But these relative riches had come too late for Bobby. He was a wreck from recurring injuries, and had to play through a pain barrier every time he went on to the pitch.

He told me how on the morning of the 1961 FA Cup Final he made two secret journeys from the team's Middlesex hotel to see his GP near his home in Palmers Green for painkilling injections on his knee. "If Bill Nicholson had known the pain I was in, he would have left me out," said Bobby. "This was the game of my life and I was determined not to miss it."

Bobby played through the pain and scored the first and laid on the second of the goals in the 2-0 victory over Leicester City that clinched that historic double.

There is a peculiar irony in the fact that the first legal betting shops in the UK were opened in May 1961, the very week that Smithy enjoyed his Wembley glory.

What few people knew is that Bobby was addicted to gambling, and betting shops became like his second home.

When Tottenham were checking out of their hotel after the away leg of their European Cup first round tie against Feyenoord in 1961-62, Bill Nick called a meeting of the players in what were pre-STD days: "Our telephone bill is 10 times what we expected," he said "Somebody has taken liberties calling home."

Bobby snapped: "All right, all right. Keep you hair on. I'll pay it when I get home."

Until this angry reaction, nobody had known that Smithy had been on the phone throughout the trip to his bookie in London.

After the Double, Bobby had two barnstorming seasons alongside Jimmy Greaves before his injuries caught up with him. He moved on to Brighton in May 1964 for £5,000.

I was interviewing Brighton manager Archie Macaulay when Smithy reported for pre-season training, and I arranged for *Daily Express* sports photographer Norman 'Speedy' Quicke to take a picture of him weighing-in on the club scales.

It was going to be just an innocent 'atmosphere' picture. Smithy had weighed 13st 9lb according to the Spurs records. Archie Macaulay hit the roof when the arrow on the scales shot up to 16st 9lb! And remember he only stood 5ft 9in. Archie told us not to print the photo, but it gave the headline writers the chance to reach for the spiteful 'Blobby' Smith puns.

It provided me with a rare exclusive and Bobby was ordered to put in extra training. He got himself in good enough shape to help shoot Brighton to the Fourth Division title before moving to

SCRAPBOOK MEMORIES: 'Blobby' Smith was a bigger star than Brighton expected when he turned up for his first training session ... three stone bigger than they expected!

Hastings for the final shots of his goal-gorged career.

As he signed off, he sold his story to the *Sunday People,* who ran the front-page banner headline: MY LIFE OF BIRDS, BOOZE AND BETTING

"I made most of it up," Bobby told me. "I was desperate for cash to clear gambling debts. But the bit about birds virtually ended my first marriage."

He became a painter and decorator and drove a minicab before the crippling injuries he had collected on the football field finally caught up with him, not helped by a fall through a manhole that damaged his already wrecked legs.

Bobby had to take a disability pension after suffering heart problems and having a hip replacement. It would have been handy if he could have sold his League championship and FA Cup winners' medals from 1961 and 1962, but they were stolen and he had the heartache of hearing how the 1961 Cup medal had turned up at an auction and sold for £11,200.

Here"s something for Spurs fans to chew on. Bobby told me: "I am always made very welcome when I go to White Hart Lane, but my first club Chelsea go further. Every Christmas they send a cheque for £1,500 to all those who were in the squad for the 1955 League championship win … and I hardly got a kick because manager Ted Drake hated my guts!"

If he had been playing today, Bobby – who mixed cruiserweight strength with subtlety on the ball – would have been revered as a player of world class, and rewarded with the riches that his ability warranted.

But he played in the soccer slave era. His rewards were pain in the limbs and – much of it self inflicted – poverty in the pocket.

Bobby scored four goals in Bill Nick's first game as Spurs manager, that 10-4 victory over Everton. Despite this performance, he was not permitted to keep the match ball, and told me: "You didn't get to keep anything in those days. I remember when I left Chelsea in 1955 I asked for a shirt, just to keep as a souvenir, and they said: "You can't have one of those, we don't have enough'."

He gave Bill plenty of headaches but for all their bust-ups they had a liking and respect for each other.

'Bill was the most disciplined and straightest man I ever knew,' Bobby told me. 'He set amazing standards of behaviour that few could meet, and his knowledge of football tactics were second to none.

"We had a lot of run-ins, but I never ever let him down on the pitch and he appreciated that. He knew that every time that first whistle blew I gave everything I had. It was punishing the way I played the game, but it was expected of centre-forwards to get stuck in. I would have found playing the modern game a doddle."

As Bill and Bobby hugged on the White Hart Lane pitch where they had known so many triumphs, there was nobody in the ground who did not have a lump in their throats.

It was clear for all to see that Bill's health was failing, and Bobby was on his way to becoming a physical wreck.

The testimonial match brought Bill a nice cheque – goodness, nearly as much as the players today earn in a week.

"Darkie and I were very grateful for the money generated by the testimonial match," BIll said, "but what meant much more than the cash was the spirit I felt in the ground, at what I thought of as my second home. It was so heartwarming to see so many of my old players. It was like being reunited with one big happy family. Martin Chivers went out of his way to make it easier for me. I'm not as mobile as I was, and without his arm to steady me I might easily have got blown over by the cheers from the crowd. I was overwhelmed."

For this night, White Hart Lane belonged to The Master.

And there was not a dry eye in the house.

Chapter Fourrteen
Tottenham's
Rock of Ages

THERE was one more hugely emotional night for Bill after his Testimonial match, when – on March 11 2004 – he was inducted as the first member of the Tottenham Hall of Fame. Snow was falling and carpeting the White Hart Lane pitch, but it's a wonder it was not melted by the warmth generated for the Master of Spurs as a sell-out audience of 300 greeted him at the convenient Paxton Road Whites suite.

Eight members of his legendary Double team from 1960-61 were there to pay tribute to him, along with 15 other players he had under his caring wing during the club's golden era.

At 85, Bill was frail and faltering as his new best friend, Martin Chivers, chaperoned him with care and undisguised affection. Chairman Daniel Levy put him perfectly in the context of the club's history when he described him as "the rock upon which Tottenham Hotspur Football Club is built." Yes, Bill was Tottenham's Rock of Ages.

Master of Ceremonies John Motson introduced the line-up of former Spurs players who had managed to get to the dinner despite the late winter weather that was refusing to recognise that spring was around the corner.

It was as if somebody had taken a pack of old football cigarette cards and tumbled them out, with the players appearing as the white-topped veterans they are today. Motty gave the roll call and each player stood and acknowledged the applause from an audience that had paid £85 a head for the privilege of being part of what was an historic night, the last public appearance of Bill Nicholson with his Super Spurs.

The history-making Double has been completed and artist Art Turner captures the lap of honour after the 2-0 defeat of Leicester City at Wembley in 1961

Tommy Harmer and Bobby Smith, who had sparkled in the famous 10-4 victory 46 years earlier, were there, along with Double team heroes Ron Henry, Maurice Norman, Dave Mackay, Cliff Jones, Les Allen, Terry Dyson, Terry Medwin and, flying in from South Africa, Peter Baker.

Also introduced were Pat Jennings, Steve Perryman, Phil Beal, John Pratt, Peter Collins, Terry Naylor, Jimmy Neighbour, John Ryden, Tony Marchi, Mel Hopkins and Eddie Clayton.

Dave Mackay, who was usually as miserly with his praise as Bill Nick, rated him 'among the six best managers in the world.' Martin Chivers conceded with something of an understatement that he'd had the odd argument with Bill, but added with a rueful grin, 'he got more out of me than any other manager could have'.

Cliff Jones, as pencil slim as in his playing days and the most dapper ex-footballer in the room, told Motty: "Bill was never just satisfied with a result. What mattered to him more was the performance. He always wanted to win, but it had to be in style. He also demanded that we represent the club with dignity. Bill would say to us that if we ever argued with a referee we should be aware that the referee knew the rules far better than we did. He hated players intimidating referees. It annoys me to see the reaction of some players today. It's quite disgraceful what some of them get up to ... the diving and cheating. Bill hated cheating of any kind. The difference in the modern game is that it's all about player-power. They are so powerful and wealthy now. In my day, we deferred to the manager. Now it's the other way round.

'To Bill, behaviour was very important. If you had misbehaved in anyway, on or off the pitch, you would inevitably hear the words you didn't want to hear from our trainer Cecil Poynton on Monday morning: 'Mr Nicholson wants to see you in his office straight away.' He would give us an earful, and God help you if you repeated the misbehaviour. But he was always fair and balanced, and gave you the chance to have your say. It was like getting told off by your Dad."

Cliffie said he believed that part of the problem in the modern game is the breakdown in relations between players and supporters. 'Bill made us very aware of our responsibility to the community," he said. "If there was an awards ceremony at a nearby boys' clubs or other clubs in the area, he'd send one of us along as representatives of Spurs. And we were happy to do it.

"I don't know what they do now, but I suspect it's not the same. We used to go into the Bell and Hare pub next to the ground after a game and talk freely with the supporters. I can't see that happening now."

Jimmy Greaves sent apologies for his absence, and in a videoed interview recalled: "One night in 1963, I was sent off for throwing a punch in retaliation during an away game against OSK Belgrade. I went straight to the dressing room, where Cecil Poynton was cleaning up.

'What are you doing here?' he asked.

'I've been sent off,' I told him.

'That's a disgrace. You've let the club down. We haven't had a player sent off since 1928.'

'And who was that? I asked.

'Me,' said Cecil.

Jim said of Bill: "The most dedicated and honest man I have ever met in football. When he was created they threw away the mould. It was a great day for me when he came to Milan to sign me. Thank you, Bill."

Throughout his career, Bill never ever came the big 'I-am'. He never wanted to to be called 'Boss' or 'Gaffer,' as Pat Jennings testified. He told Motty how nervous he was when he first met 'Mr. Nicholson' at Watford when he was just 18. He immediately put me at my ease by insisting on being addressed as 'Bill' and not 'Mister Nicholson'. He was 'Bill' to everybody.

Steve Perryman, who went from sixteen-year-old apprentice under his mentor to skipper and player with most club appearances, said: "Bill is respected throughout the world, not just in the British game. Almost every week there were foreign journalists and coaches dropping into our Cheshunt training ground to get some tips on tactics and match preparation. He always had fresh ideas but never complicated things. His motto was 'keep it simple, do it the Spurs way.' Everybody who played under him became an improved player by following his advice."

Peter Baker, who had flown in from his home in Durban, said: "I would not have missed this for the world. Bill helped all of we players have the best and most successful times of our lives. We could not have pulled off the Double without his meticulous planning. We owe him so much."

Fellow Yorkshireman Terry Dyson bowed as he shook Bill's hand. "I was always in awe of you," he said. "You've mellowed but I bet you could still get us running our hearts out for you."

Comedian Bobby Davro conducted an auction that raised £8,000 for the Tottenham in the Community charity, and told Bill: "I am a lifetime Spurs fan and am in awe of all you achieved for our club. I know I am speaking on behalf of all supporters when I say thank you, thank you, thank you for all that you did for Tottenham. You gave us that precious thing called pride, and set the standards that all your successors have had to try to meet. You have given them all an impossible act to follow."

Bill was formally presented with an inscribed crystal glass decanter, and despite his obvious weakness he insisted on giving emotion-charged thanks to his players and all present for maintaining the spirit of Tottenham.

All in the audience were fighting back tears as a standing ovation was followed by a rendition of the 'Glory, Glory' anthem and 'For He's A Jolly Good Fellow.'

Then Bill, aided by Martin Chivers, walked slowly off into the winter's night.

Everybody in the room felt privileged to have been there on this special night, because they knew as well as saying thank you to Mr Tottenham they were also saying goodbye.

Chapter Fifteen
A Manager's Manager

WITHIN seven months of the Tottenham Hall of Fame induction and after moving with Darkie to a warden-assisted flat in the Arsenal territory of Potters Bar, Bill passed on at the end of a life devoted to football in general and Spurs in particular. He died on the morning of Saturday October 23 2004 at the age of 85, and in the afternoon Tottenham were beaten 2-1 at home by Bolton Wanderers. Many grown men (and women) cried when his death was announced. The Lane was awash with tears.

The tributes to a simple yet great man came tumbling in by the bucket load. I gathered many of them in my freelancing role for several newspapers and media outlets, and added more following the emotional memorial service staged at White Hart Lane on Sunday, September 7 2004, where the loyal, loving Darkie and daughters, Linda and Jean, led the mourners, with son-in-law Steve Bell giving a moving oration on behalf of the family.

Spurs chairman Daniel Levy captured the mood of the 8,000 congregation at the Lane when he said: "Bill's passing is a tragedy for the whole of football but particularly so for his family and all of us at Spurs. He was loved by everyone at White Hart Lane and there is no doubt that he in turn loved this club.

"Bill devoted his whole life to Tottenham Hotspur and to our fans, and will never be surpassed as the greatest individual in our history. He lifted Spurs from mediocrity to the sublime as we became the first British club to win a European trophy and to so many wonderful achievements such as that special Double of 1960-61. He will never be forgotten."

On the following pages, in no particular order, are many of the quotes made at the time of Bill's death from eyewitnesses to his remarkable career, with the portraits penned and pencilled by renowned artist Art Turner:

MR SPURS, FIRST MODERN BOSS TO WIN THE DOUBLE, DIES AT 85

Bill Nick – a gent and one of the true greats

By Jim Holden

BILL NICHOLSON, the last survivor of the golden age of football managers, died peacefully yesterday. He was 85.

He was called The Gentleman Manager and was perhaps less well-known, possibly because he didn't have the showman swagger and voluble style of rivals like Bill Shankly and Brian Clough.

But Nicholson ranks alongside all of them, Shankly and Jock Stein included, as one of the greatest men of British football.

His glory, Tottenham team of the early 1960s, was the first of modern times to win The Double. They were the first club from these shores to win a European trophy, a feat he achieved three times in total.

And, even more memorable than the success, was the way his Spurs team, created by Nicholson, played what is still considered to be the most beautiful football of any champion team.

In his first match as manager at White Hart Lane, his side won 10-4 against Everton.

Bill Nick demanded style above all else, and brought the players to deliver it – from Danny Blanchflower, John White and Dave Mackay to Jimmy Greaves, Alan Mullery and Martin Peters.

Mullery yesterday recalled the insistence on entertainment, saying:

We used to get rollickings if we didn't play with style

to live in a modest house a few streets away from White Hart Lane.

So much so, that when he tempted Greaves to return home from an unhappy spell in Italy, he refused to break the £100,000 transfer barrier.

Comparisons are fruitless, but they were certainly made to decide the finest single side of the English game.

GOODBYE BILL: Tottenham players remember Nicholson against Bolton yesterday and (inset right) Jewell lowers outside White Hart Lane before the funeral and (far left) Bill Nick in his great Double-winning Spurs side in 1961

one appearance for England as a wing-half against Portugal. He scored on his debut, but was never picked again.

Instead, he made his indelible mark as a manager. Many good judges claim his Glory Glory team that won The Double in season 1960/1 was the finest side of the English game.

Comparisons are fruitless, but they were certainly made to decide the finest single side of the English game, as rivals the current invincibles

of Arsenal. They won the FA Cup the following year, too, and then the European Cup Winners' Cup in 1963. Another FA Cup followed in 1967, as two UEFA Cup triumphs and two UEFA Cup triumphs.

It was in that last final, against Feyenoord in 1974, that Nicholson's love affair with football turned sour.

Hooligan rioting among Spurs fans at the game in Rotterdam led to more than 200 injuries. As violence continued Nicholson took the microphone to appeal for calm over the public address system. His anger and disgust spilled out in the now famous

comment: "You people make me feel ashamed to be an Englishman." And ashamed to be a man of football.

A few months later he resigned from Spurs and was only later to have a working relationship again, in his early fifties, but The Gentleman Manager could no longer sit comfortably away from the club.

Nicholson, though, continued to watch the club which had captured his heart. He was chief scout, a consultancy role eventually given from his home until illness intervened.

He remained forever the humble hero, a genius of football, and among the greatest of all football managers.

GENIUS: Nicholson

SCRAPBOOK MEMORIES: *White Hart Lane was swimming in tears the day that Bill Nicholson, Mr Spurs, passed on. He died, aged 85, on the morning of Saturday October 23 2004. In the afternoon the Spurs and Bolton players joined first of all in silent tribute, and when his face appeared on the jumbo screens the cheers and applause could be heard all the way down Bill Nicholson Way to Creighton Road and up in the heavens.*

DAVE MACKAY

Rated by Bill Nick as arguably his best buy when he bought him from Hearts in 1959. Bill made him his captain following the retirement of Danny Blanchflower, and he collected the FA Cup in 1967.

'Bill was not only a brilliant manager, but also a perfect gentleman. He gave me the privilege of captaining his team, and it was my honour to play for him. What people didn't see was the human side of him, quietly encouraging me when I was out of the game with a twice-broken leg. He kept assuring me there was a place for me when I was fit. He didn't give praise easily. You had to earn it. He could come down on you like a ton of bricks if he felt you had given less than your best. There was no better judge of a player, and his tactics were always designed to be positive. Bill did not have a negative bone in his body. He was an out-and-out perfectionist and I remember him being disappointed after we had clinched the Double in the 1961 FA Cup Final. Bill was proud of what we had achieved but frustrated that we had not played nearly as well as we could. That was Bill. He always wanted the best for Tottenham and the supporters. I was lucky to play under two of the greatest managers in Bill and Brian Clough. They were both Yorkshiremen but completely contrasting as men and managers in the way they went about things. Both were born winners and masters at motivating players. Brian went last month, and now Bill. They are irreplaceable. We will not see their like again.'

ALAN MULLERY

Signed by Bill from Fulham in 1964 as replacement for Danny Blanchflower. Captained the Tottenham team that won the 1972 Uefa Cup and famously did a solo lap of honour round a pitch crammed with celebrating fans.

'One word sums up Bill as a football manager: Genius. Nobody read a game better than Bill, and he had a photographic memory of just about every opponent we faced. He could tell you the strengths and weaknesses of all the players. A test of a manager is what long-serving players think of him. I arrived at White Hart Lane when most of the Double-winning team were still playing, and the esteem in which he was held by them was unbelievable. Bill always gave it to you straight. He did not give false praise, and was quick to tell you when you did something wrong. Even in victory he would keep his feet on the ground and look for the things that needed tightening and improving. I remember a game when we beat Burnley 4-0 and he gave us a rollocking because some of our play was loose and undisciplined. Bill didn't suffer fools, and gave all his concentration and time to the team and the club. He was always described as being dour, but he often had a twinkle in his eye and could be humorous in his own way. He will be remembered as one of the greatest managers of all time, and I considered myself very lucky to have played under him. If you ever got a pat on the back from Bill then you knew you had done something special. He will always be a legend at Tottenham.'

STEVE PERRYMAN

Bill Nick gave him his debut at the age of seventeen in 1969, and Steve went on to become the most selected player in the club's history. He played 854 first-team games, including a record 655 League matches.

'Back in the days when I was a schoolboy footballer in West London, the odds were on me joining Queen's Park Rangers. But from the moment I met Bill Nicholson I knew that he was the manager and Tottenham were the club for me. Bill Nick was the most honest man to cross my path, either in or out of football. He did not offer me any illegal inducements to sign for Spurs, just his word that he would treat me fairly and that he would make sure I got the best possible coaching support. Tell a lie ... I suppose the tickets he offered to me and my parents to watch the 1967 FA Cup final between Tottenham and Chelsea could be called an inducement. From the moment I saw the great Dave Mackay lift the Cup for Spurs I knew I was going to join them. I never dreamed then that I would go on to play a record number of games for the club. In those days it was very much a family club, with Bill Nick surrounding himself with a staff of likeable, friendly people who were Spurs through and through. He gave fantastic service to the club, and never with any selfish thoughts. All he wanted was what was best for Tottenham. In fact he *was* Tottenham. There has been nobody who has given greater service to the club, and he set sky-high standards for those who followed in his path.'

PAT JENNINGS

Joined Spurs from Watford in 1964 and developed into one of the world's great goalkeepers, and was forgiven by Spurs fans for later taking his great talent to that other team in North London.

'When you think of Tottenham you automatically think of Bill Nicholson - one of the legendary figures in football. He was like a father figure to me, and probably the biggest influence on my life. When I first arrived from Watford I was young and inexperienced and had a bit of a wobbly time. But Bill stood by me and gave me the confidence I needed with his quiet words of encouragement and advice. His knowledge of football was second to none, and when he spoke about the game it came right from the heart. He'd been there, done that and so you listened with respect. He expected everybody to share his total commitment to Spurs and anybody who gave less than his best in the Tottenham jersey was going to get an earful. He could make players shake with his criticism, which was always constructive. Bill set the highest principles and expected his players to perform in a sporting yet competitive way. At all times he preached that the game should be kept simple and direct. He despised cheating in any form and never looked to take short cuts to success. I remember he hated the way the game went very defensive in the 1970s. He thought football should be attractive and entertaining to watch. Tottenham were so lucky to have him at the helm, and he was without doubt one of the greatest managers the game has ever seen.'

JIMMY GREAVES

Bill bought Jimmy for what was then a record £99,999 from Milan in 1960, and he responded by scoring a club record 220 League goals for Tottenham. He scored 44 goals in 57 England internationals.

‘You always knew where you stood with Bill, and I would rate him the greatest bloke I ever worked for. He knew which players needed a kick up the arse, and which needed an arm around the shoulder. So many people in football say one thing and mean another. Bill was always straight and he said what he meant. He could be a miserable sod at times, but that's what the pressure of management does to you. Once you got to know the real Bill Nick you found a warm, generous and totally trustworthy man. I used to watch him play when I was a kid and he was a true 100 per center who never gave anything less than his best on the pitch. And that was how he was as a manager, always pouring himself into his job. He expected the same attitude and effort from his players. It's well known that I was never a fan of coaches, but Bill kept it simple and you knew what he wanted from you. No mumbo jumbo. Spurs paid him poorly and did not give him the sort of rewards he deserved for making them one of the most attractive teams in Europe. I couldn't believe it when they let him go, but Keith Burkinshaw had the sense to bring him back in a scouting and consultancy role. He had one of the best brains in football, and he was totally committed to Tottenham. Bill had blue and white blood and always put the club at the top of his agenda. ’

CLIFF JONES

Signed from Swansea in 1958, Cliff was a prominent member of the Double side and scored 135 goals in 318 League games. A winger who could play on either flank, he was capped 59 times by Wales.

‘Bill would rarely praise a player because he thought that bred complacency. He always wanted us on our toes and not thinking we were the finished product. I remember feeling really pleased with myself after playing what I thought was a good game. As I waited for Bill's praise he said, 'Don't forget, son, that a pat on the back is only a couple of feet away from a kick up the backside.' He rarely swore. He left that to Eddie Baily, who could swear for Britain. There has never been a manager who paid such attention to detail. At our team talks he would go through the opposition with a fine tooth comb. His knowledge of every player was amazing, and he used to tell us how to play to make the most of the opposition weaknesses and would warn about their strengths. He managed the club from the bootroom to the boardroom, and would never take any interference from the directors. They had such confidence in him that they left him to get on with it. He always insisted that the most important people at the club were the supporters and that we should feel privileged to play for them. I have never known a manager have as much time for the fans, and he always made a point of talking and, more important, listening to them. Time and again he would tell us to play for the supporters because they paid our wages. He will be desperately missed by everybody connected with the club.’

GLENN HODDLE

Arguably the most skilful Tottenham player in history, who played 499 League and cup games for Spurs and scored 110 goals before taking his talent to Monaco. Capped 53 times by England.

•I was lucky to play under Bill as a youngster but he had resigned by the time I made my League debut. I was in awe of him, and when I was a boy learning the game I considered him one of the greatest of all the managers. Nothing ever changed my mind. He was Mr Tottenham Hotspur and everything the club stands for emanated from Bill, who laid the foundations and gave the club pride and belief in itself. He always remained totally dedicated to Spurs. He had presence, he knew what he wanted, he knew how his team should and would function. He was a manager who truly managed. It was Bill more than anybody who established the traditions of Tottenham Hotspur Football Club. He never tried to complicate the game, and he always sent his teams out to be positive. A little anecdote that shows what a perfectionist he was: I once scored a hat-trick in a youth match that Bill was watching. Obviously I was feeling pretty pleased with myself. He came to me in the dressing-room afterwards and said, 'Young man, you were lucky to get that third goal of yours. It should have been a pass to a player in a better position.' And I knew in my heart he was right, and it taught me a lesson. You must play for the team, not for yourself. Bill did not want flashy, show-off individualists. He wanted a team working together. That's how he built his great Double side, with the emphasis on teamwork. No question about it, Bill was the Master.•

MARTIN CHIVERS

Signed for Spurs from Southampton in 1968 for what was then a Football League record fee of £125,000. He scored 118 goals in 278 League games, and netted 13 goals in 24 international games for England.

'Bill and I had several ups and downs because I believed in speaking my mind, but we finished up the best of friends. My biggest beef was that he could never find it within himself to give us praise when we deserved it. He seemed to find it really hard to bring himself to say 'well done lads.' Typical of him was that after one victory over Wolves he went into their dressing-room and commiserated with them and then came into our dressing-room where we were celebrating our win and gave us a going-over for our performance. I cannot think of any other manager who would have done that, perhaps with the exception of Brian Clough. Bill was brutally honest when sometimes it would have been better not to say anything. His record speaks for itself. He was one of the finest managers ever, as I often told him after he and I had retired. The club paid him peanuts and I used to argue that he should have got we players better terms. But he was never driven by profit. He just wanted a perfect team and was always looking to build another 'Double' side. Neither of us enjoyed our last season together, but these things happen and if I could turn the clock back I would probably have been less argumentative. I am just happy we made up. He was a good man, for whom I had the greatest respect and I got on famously with his lovely wife, Darkie.'

TERRY MEDWIN

Despite a succession of injuries, he managed to score 65 goals in 197 League games for Spurs after joining them from Swansea as a cultured right winger. He won 30 caps with Wales until a broken leg cut short his career.

'Bill was way ahead of his time in terms of coaching. When I arrived from Wales, I was used to doing training which was dominated by running and continual laps of the pitch, but he was doing things which most clubs hadn't even thought of. He insisted on a lot of ball work to go with our fitness training, and he made every player really think about his game and his personal contribution to each match. He also had a lovely manner with the players and treated us as individuals and that helped us to blend as a team. There was mutual respect. Bill lived a life which revolved around Tottenham Hotspur, the club coming first at all times. Nobody had a bad word to say about him because he was a gentleman. He was always asking after my kids, and was a really caring, warm man under that dour Yorkshire exterior. I can never recall him trying to claim the spotlight at the expense of his players, and he would always treat everybody with respect. Even when he was giving you a rollocking you could not take offence because you knew he was doing it for all the right reasons. When I went into coaching, I took a lot of Bill with me. He showed that coaching should be inspirational and not boring or bewildering. I can hear him saying, 'Keep it simple ...' Tottenham Hotspur will never have a more loyal and conscientious servant.'

GARY MABBUTT

It was in his role as chief scout that Bill discovered Gary Mabbutt when he was a virtual unknown at Bristol Rovers. He played 477 League games for Tottenham and captained the 1991 FA Cup winners despite the handicap of diabetes.

•Bill had a special aura about him, and I was proud to have him giving me fatherly advice when I was transferred to Tottenham on his recommendation. He was up there with Bill Shankly, Sir Matt Busby and Sir Alf Ramsey for being respected throughout the game. He had forgotten more than I knew about the game, and I was privileged to listen to him talking about football and the way Spurs liked to do things. I remember shaking with excitement when he invited me to meet him for transfer talks. When we came face to face for the first time, I said nervously: 'Hello, Mr Nicholson, I'm Gary Mabutt.' He shook my hand and said, 'Call me Bill.' He immediately put me at my ease and did not come the big I-am. He won me over easily and I had no hesitation in signing for the club. I never regretted it and I am so grateful that Bill talked me into it. One of the main thrusts of his talk to me was that players should live the right kind of life, and respect their bodies. I felt fortunate to have such a great man giving me sound advice that I always tried to follow. When I won a lifetime achievement award from the Professional Footballers' Association I was honoured to have it presented to me by Bill, who deservedly got the biggest ovation of the night. Everybody in the game thought the world of him. He was quite simply a legend.•

JOE KINNEAR

Joined Tottenham from St Albans City in 1965 and was right-back in Tottenham's 1967 FA Cup winning team. Played 192 League games for Spurs and won 26 Republic of Ireland caps.

⁶I had more than ten years as a Tottenham player under Bill and could not have wished to play for a better manager. Every day working with him was like an education. He was a great manager, an even greater coach. I can still hear his wise words in my head when I am out on the training ground as a manager myself today. I was brought up at Tottenham to train with the ball on the ground and I continue to use many of Bill's methods. Be first, be accurate, play the way you're facing, get into position when you're not in possession, when the ball is dead come alive. All these simple instructions are going through my head as I think of Bill and the training sessions we used to have at Cheshunt. Today's players won't go far wrong if they do things Bill's way because it's the right way. The club treated him really badly when they let him go in 1974, but thank goodness they made amends by taking him back as a scout and consultant. Tottenham was his life and it was cruel for him when he was virtually forced away from the club, and I am so glad they eventually took him back. Ask anybody who played under him and they will only have good things to say. He was a hard taskmaster, but that's the way it has to be if you are to get the right discipline and enthusiasm from your players. Bill could always get the best out of us. It was a privilege to have had him as my manager.⁹

MARTIN PETERS

Moved to Tottenham as the first £200,000 footballer in 1970, with Jimmy Greaves going to West Ham as a £54,000 makeweight in the transfer. An elegant member of England's 1966 World Cup winners.

•It was the lure of playing for Bill that made me decide to join Spurs from West Ham. Everybody in the game admired him and his achievements. He would encourage us to go out and play the way we had been brought up to play, with the emphasis on pure football. This was good for me because I was used to a similar style at West Ham. Bill and Hammers manager Ron Greenwood were good friends and shared the same outlook on the game. It had to be played properly, with style and skill. Bill was a football man from the top of his head to the tip of his toes, and he could be considered the manager's manager. He was a major servant to English football and a fantastic man. I always found him honest and fair and willing to listen if you had a point you wanted to put across. I honestly considered it an honour to serve under him. It was easy to see that he and Alf Ramsey had played with each other for Tottenham, because they had the same perfectionist standards and believed in keeping the game simple yet positive. Bill's passing is a sad day for football and in particular for Tottenham, the club to which he was completely devoted and dedicated. He will be sadly missed but always warmly remembered by all those who had the privilege of playing for him. There is no doubt that he was one of the great English football managers and I felt so lucky to have become his captain at Spurs.•

PHIL BEAL

Played 420 League and cup games for Spurs after signing from school in 1960, turning professional in 1962. A versatile defender, he played in the '71 and '73 League Cup winning teams and also the '74 Uefa Cup final.

'It used to be a joke among the lads that I was always the first name on Bill's team-sheet. Eddie Baily assured me it was true, and I was one of the few players who used to get a regular 'well done' from Bill who was famously mean with his praise. I thought the world of him and always found him a fair man who made sense with his assessments of your performance. I can think of few people who could match his coaching knowledge. He could come up with tactics to suit any situation, and knew exactly how to exploit any team's weaknesses. How he did not get a knighthood is a disgrace. He was up there with the very best managers like Busby, Shankly, Ramsey and Clough. Those people who described him as dour did not really know him. He had a good sense of humour and liked to have laughter in the dressing-room when the time was right. I got up to a lot of pranks and he saw it as good for team spirit. He always demanded that we went out of our way to recognise the support of our fans. I was at the dinner where he was made the first Life Member of the Hall of Fame, and I realised then that he was looking frail, but it still came as a shock when he died. It's difficult to imagine Spurs without Bill Nicholson. He was Mr Tottenham and gave his heart and soul to the club. I felt privileged to have played for him. He was a wonderful man.'

JOHN PRATT

Scored 49 goals from midfield in 415 League and Cup games from 1965 to 1979. He played in virtually every outfield position, but was at his most effective when playing an anchorman role in midfield.

*•*I don't mind admitting that I cried the day Martin Chivers rang me to tell me that Bill had died. He was such an important figure in my life. He WAS Tottenham Hotspur Football Club in my eyes. Bill treated us all like one big family. He had no favourites and rollocked us all equally! He demanded our very best efforts at all times and was quick to come down on anybody giving less than his best. Bill could forgive almost anything except lack of total commitment. I used to get quite a lot of stick from some sections of the Tottenham crowd and it would have been easy to get disheartened, but the fact that Bill had faith in me and kept selecting me did wonders for my confidence. If I was satisfying Bill I knew I must have been doing something right because he was an out and out perfectionist. Bill was up there with Shankly for having a great relationship with the fans. He always found time to talk to them and was happy to listen to their point of view. He used to tell us in his team talks how important the supporters were. "They pay your wages," he would say. "They are entitled to criticise because they've paid to come in. Now go out and entertain them." He not only wanted us to win matches, but to do it in what he called 'Spurs style.' The day Bill died a bit of Tottenham died with him. There will never be another Bill Nicholson.*•*

GARY LINEKER

•It's impossible to put on a Spurs shirt without knowing the Bill Nicholson legend. He WAS Tottenham Hotspur, a man who gave much of his life to service to the club. A manager of great dignity and pride, he always wanted things done properly and with style. I was born in the famous Spurs Double season, and what he achieved with that wonderful team is part of football history. Everything since at Spurs has been measured by that feat.•

ROY HODGSON

•Bill represented all that was best about English football. When I first came into the game as a kid with Crystal Palace he was top of the tree with Tottenham, who had just become the first winners of a major European tophy. Everybody in the game looked up to him, and he set the standards all the other managers tried to match. He had the highest moral values and expected his players to perform not only with skill but with sportsmanship. Yes, he deserved a knightood.•

SIR ALEX FERGUSON

•There is not a manager from my generation who does not respect and admire all that Bill Nicholson achieved. He was famously a fan of Scottish football and players and I remember we young pros were in awe of his Double success in 1960-61. When I became a manager I had in mind the standards set by the likes of Bill, Sir Matt Busby, Jock Stein and Bill Shankly. They liked to win in style, and I used that as my yardstick.•

DAVID PLEAT

•Bill was a hard task master who expected the players to do the job they were paid for, to play with movement and style and with harmony. For 16 years that harmonious rhythm was the personification of Spurs. Under Bill's baton they were like a well-tuned orchestra, all playing for each other. He was down to earth, blunt, tough but fair; an exceptionally hardworking and knowledgeable man. His wonderful work and achievements for Tottenham will not be equalled.•

MARTIN JOL

'The name of Bill Nicholson is known and highly respected throughout European football. It was my privilege to be at his memorial service when I was able to bow the knee to the greatest of all Tottenham managers. For all those of us who have had the honour of following in his path, he set impossible standards! He always insisted on the game being played not only skilfully but also fairly. The Nicholson way was the right way.'

HARRY REDKNAPP

'There've been few better British managers in the history of football. When I took over at Spurs I knew I was not fit to tie Bill's bootlaces, but I tried to follow his beliefs in providing football that was not only effective but also entertaining. Bill never sent out a team to bore, and he considered the supporters the most important people in the club. He was always a favourite with the Redknapp family, including my Dad and Jamie. We recognised true class when we saw it.'

TERRY VENABLES

'There is nobody in the game who has a bad word to say about Bill. He played a big part in my life by taking me to Spurs from Chelsea. I always found him straight and at times savagely honest. He had a clear vision of how he wanted the game played, and touched perfection with the Double team. His unselfish service to Spurs was astonishing, and he set the bar ridiculously high for all his successors. Follow that!'

KEN FRIAR

'I was privileged to represent Arsenal at Bill's memorial service. We were rivals for many years, but I never had anything but total respect for a man who always sought football of a high and honest standard. His great Double team of 1960-61 was one of the untouchable sides, and it encouraged us to equal the achievement ten years later. I found Bill a quietly dignified man, who never allowed our rivalry to boil over into any sort of enmity. He was a thorough gentleman.'

TOMMY DOCHERTY

'For much of my career, Bill was a rival but never once did he have anything less than my full respect. It was always a special challenge when I was facing his team because I knew I was crossing swords with the tactical master. I particularly remember walking out with him at Wembley for the 1967 FA Cup final, and after Spurs had beaten Chelsea he was almost sympathetic. They don't make them like Bill anymore.'

JOHN MOTSON

'It was my honour to MC the night when Bill became the first member of the Tottenham Hall of Fame. It was his last public appearance, and the love for him in the room was almost palpable. I commentated on many of his outstanding matches, and his teams always reflected the man ... honest in their endeavour and determined to win in the right spirit and style. I would rate him in the top six British managers of all time, and he was comfortably the most honest.'

JOHN BOND

•I learned so much from Bill, both by watching his teams and from sitting at his feet listening. When I was a player with West Ham I used to go out of my way to watch Spurs play, because they were easily the best team in town. Later on I used to pick Bill's brains and he was such a generous man, readily giving advice and opinions. He was a humble, modest man who had lots to boast about. I was really fond of him and his wife Darkie. •

KEITH BURKINSHAW

•Bill was light years ahead with his tactical knowledge. He was a master at knowing how to get his players to make use of space on the pitch. I was delighted to welcome him back into the Spurs family. It was like coming home for him. He never ever interfered but was always ready and willing to give expert advice when asked. For Bill, football was always a sport, a game to be played with imagination and commitment. He hated the greed element, because it was against all his principles.•

RON ATKINSON

•When I first started out as a manager I wanted to learn from the best, and the man I approached, of course, was Bill Nicholson. He willingly gave me time and advice and allowed me to pick his brains. People used to say he was dour, but I found him far from being that way. He loved talking football and was really illuminating and his eyes would sparkle as he talked about how the game should always be played with style.'

BOB WILSON

•Despite my Arsenal background, I got to know Bill and his wonderful wife Darkie really well. In my role as chairman of the London Football Coaches' Association I used to welcome Bill to our meetings and he always got the biggest cheer of the night when introduced. He was a modest man who had lots to shout about, but let his achievements speak for themselves. Few could match his knowledge of football tactics. This Gooner was privileged to know him.'

Extra Time
*Fan mail
for Bill Nick*

THROUGHOUT his career, Bill considered the fans the most important people in the game. He regularly used to tell his players: "Never ever take them for granted. They pay your wages … go out and entertain them."

He subscribed to the romantic Danny Blanchflower view:

It is better to fail aiming high than to succeed aiming low. And we of Spurs have set our sights very high, so high in fact that even failure will have in it an echo of glory.

That is a quote often attributed to Bill, but it actually came from the lips of the poet Blanchflower rather than the pragmatist Nicholson, who – as anybody who knew him well will confirm – never used to speak like that. He was pure, blunt-and-to-the-point Yorkshire, while Danny was the one who used to talk with the tongue and thoughts of a visionary. He made this statement in 1963, at the height of Tottenham's glory-glory status, and somehow it has been transferred to Bill Nick. He did not have the time or patience for flowery speech. He was only interested in getting the job done, and was never ever guilty of confusing his players with his pre-match instructions.

The loyalty and respect that Bill Nick showed the supporters was a two-way street, and it was returned in spades by the Tottenham faithful, who appreciated his love of the club to which he had devoted so much of his life.

When I was preparing this book I went on line and invited Facebook and Twitter followers to join in the tributes. Here is a selection of their contributions:

DAVID GUTHRIE Wokingham, Berks

The record books tell me that the home match in question with Sheffield Wednesday took place on 16th January 1993. The game itself has little or no significance in my life. It was, however, a chance meeting with a legendary figure in the history of Tottenham Hotspur on the way to the ground that will forever be a treasured memory.

Accompanied by my then 13-year-old son, Steve, we followed our usual path to White Hart Lane, which took us down Creighton Road. In the midst of some idle chatter, I suddenly caught sight of Bill Nicholson leaving his house and saying goodbye to his wife, Darkie.

We were almost level with his front garden. The dilemma now facing me was whether I should interrupt him leaving his side gate to go around to his car or let him be in peace. In a split second I decided that since there was hardly anyone else around and the chance may never arise again, to go for it. I shouted 'Ok Bill?' with a thumbs-up sign and he smiled and nodded. At the same time, Darkie beckoned me to come over to view a new heavy sweatshirt that she was wearing with a print of Bill in his prime as the Spurs manager. At the same time I was able to shake hands with him, as a thousand memories going back to my first match in 1962 rushed through my mind in the process. 'Oh Mr Nicholson' I thought, 'there are so many things I would love to say to you!' And then, he was gone with a wave as he made his way down to his car. It was brief, but for me pure magic.

My Son then said to me 'who was that old guy Dad?' Oh Stevie, son, have I got a story to tell you!

IAN PAWLEY London

I was born in 1973 so was too young to remember Bill. My first match was the 1981 FA Cup final when I was seven. When I heard the name of Bill Nicholson I asked my Dad about him. "Son," he said, "imagine Christmas without Santa.. That would be Spurs without Bill Nick."

KEVIN BUZEC Hoddesdon, Herts

When I was a young boy about 9 or 10 years old I often used to reluctantly go shopping with my nan and late granddad to our local Sainsburys on Tottenham High Road. Several times I recall my granddad talking to "some old man" at the checkouts whilst packing the shopping. When I asked him and my nan about who it was, all I remember being told is he was something to do with Spurs. If only I knew then what I know now, that the "some old man" was the legend Bill Nicholson.

I can't begin to imagine what it must have been like for my granddad to meet what must have been a true hero of his, speaking about Double wins and the true glory days of my granddad's era.

What I would give now to see him talking football with my granddad whilst packing the shopping away.

What a real legend of our glorious game you are Bill. Your opinions, ideas and outlook on our game will never be forgotten!

ALAN PAPWORTH Norwich

The one noticeable comment that comes up frequently about Bill by his peers and the players that he managed appears to be his honesty. I also believe he was not a praiseworthy man and any that was said was valued indeed. Bill carried on the traditions of good football instilled by Arthur Rowe during his time and the Spurs were always under his guidance an entertaining team, with Bill always looking to carry on that with the players he brought in. I had the pleasure of meeting him once as a youth wandering around the front entrance out of season whilst visiting a grandmother who lived nearby. He asked what I was doing there, never mentioning who he was (although I knew) and proceeded to chat shyly I thought about the ground almost in a caretaker's way, asking me also if I played all in a non patronising manner.

FRANK RANKIN Edinburgh

I am a proud Scot and recognise that Bill Nicholson was extraordinary. His playing and management career coupled with his love of Tottenham were second to none, and he is without doubt the man who made Spurs a great club. Truly great.

I used to go to Tynecastle and played there sometimes. I'd go with my Dad who used to tell me all about the Hearts team of the late 50s and early 60s. That was some team and we used to wonder how they would have got on against Bill Nicholson's Spurs that won the Double in the year that I was born.

Maybe Hearts would have won if Dave Mackay put his maroon shirt back on. It would have been that close.

Bill Nicholson goes down as the greatest and most loyal player, manager and outstanding person to have represented Tottenham Hotspur. He was a giant of the game and in my opinion ranks alongside the four great Scots, Busby, Shankly, Stein and Ferguson. I can give him no higher praise. Bill Nicholson is a total legend.

JOHNNY MARKS Southsea, Hampshire

Bill was the manager when I first started supporting Tottenham. In that time he built the greatest ever Spurs sides, though I only ever saw 'live' the last phases from 1967-74 so missed the true glory he brought to N17 both on the pitch and in the trophy cabinet. He remains the greatest of all leaders of the club and instilled in Tottenham the finest traditions. I believe that Keith Burkinshaw understood what to aspire to, and did well, whilst Harry Redknapp and Martin Jol had a fair crack at emulating a true 'great'. Bill deserves greater recognition for all he did domestically and in Europe, but I will always remember him with affection and for bringing the club the 'Glory,Glory Days', the like of which I may never experience again.

JOHN MASSIE Hitchin, Herts

Mr Tottenham!

Too young to witness what you achieved at Spurs,

But proud to follow the club that you built.

You are part of the very fabric of our glorious and historical club.

Me and my brother went to the Lane to pay our respects when you passed away, and it was a day neither of us will ever ever forget.

A sea of people,flowers, shirts, scarves

All kinds or tributes to our Bill.

Masses of fans paying their respect, consoling each other and queuing up to sign the book of condolences.

Young and old generations of fans, there for the same reason,and there for each other.

Gave me goosebumps like never before.

Felt every emotion following Spurs,

But never ever felt that feeling like that day.

That's when it truly hit me why we call you Mr Tottenham.

The club that Bill made.

TERRY HILL North London

In 1973, the *Tottenham Herald* asked young supporters to write about their favourite player. Aged 14 I wrote about John Pratt. I won the competition. The prize - meet Bill Nick and my hero John at White Hart Lane. We – my Dad and I – met them at the underground training pitch where Bill presented me with an autographed ball. He took the time to show us the training pitch.

When John Pratt joined us, Bill summoned Keith Osgood to fetch the ball to be signed. No questions asked, Keith immediately ran to collect the ball. Would a modern day player do likewise?

My Dad, a supporter since 1949, said how down to earth Bill was, with time for everybody. He gave this young Spurs fan a priceless memory, and I treasure the photograph that was taken.

Terry Hill's precious memory captured for ever as his hero John Pratt signs a ball supervised by The Master, Bill Nicholson

MIKE WESTWOOD Coseley, West Midlands

11th October 1958, Wolves had just beaten a post Munich Manchester United 4-0 at the Molineux. Our bus stop was outside a barber's shop in Wolverhampton and at five o'clock the familiar tune that heralded the start of *Sports Report* blared out.

As a Wolves fan, I was expecting programme presenter Eamonn Andrews to eulogise on the Wolves result, but no, it was Tottenham Hotspur 10 Everton 4 that were the headlines. Two mediocre teams at the time had produced a feast of football and a result that I don't think has ever been bettered. It was Bill Nicholson's first match in charge and because I was an impressionable football mad 9 year old Tottenham became a team whose result I would look for every week, but ultimately because of Bill's skill in managing and picking players became extremely jealous of three years later.

The side that Nick developed was, even for a Wolves fan that had been brought up on year in year out success, a joy to behold, the hardness of Mackay, the silky skills of John White, the battering ram that was Bobby Smith. They played Wolves on April the 23rd 1960, Wolves were still a very good side, Spurs beat us 3-1, no they didn't just beat us they annihilated us, even more so than Barcelona had done a few months previously, the week after we beat Chelsea at the Bridge 5-1, but the damage had been done; the result cost us the League.

The rest is history, Tottenham under Bill went on to do the "double" and become a force in British football under a man who in my eyes, very much like Stanley Cullis, is a forgotten "Master" of the simple game of football. Bill was a true football man.

THE MAUREENS, TURNER Chingford/**CARPENTER** Cornwall

Bill Nicholson was a true gentleman. We used to see him and his wife Darkie in Sainsburys in Tottenham High Road. He always had time to stop and chat to people, when they recognised him (which was all the time) and he was always so polite.

Back in the 70s our family had an allotment in Creighton

Road, and my mum, dad, sister and her husband and we cousin Maureens would all be over there. Bill had the allotment that backed on to his garden and we had to walk past it to ours. Both Bill and Darkie would always stop to chat and ask how we were getting on. He never had any airs or graces, and as well as being remembered as our best manager, I think the people of Tottenham took him to their hearts because he never acted as if he was any better then anybody else and Tottenham always remained his home.

TONY ODDEN Chelmsford, Essex

Sir or not ...Sir Bill Nick is Mr Tottenham Hotspur, from Boot boy to the club's most successful manager in its entire history. Bill will always be remembered as one of the true greats of the game. 'Sir Bill' never to be forgotten.

My one and only own personal memory of him was back in the late 80's. I was a cocky young boy who thought I knew everything there is to know about Spurs. I was standing next to a man who offered his opinion about the team with which I disagreed. My thoughts were, 'what do you know about Spurs?' But I respected the man and thought what a lovely friendly gentleman. You've guessed it. Yes, it was 'Sir Bill' standing directly under the road sign Bill Nicholson Way. How silly did I feel when I realized who it was! It is a memory that continues to warm me to this day.

NIKHIL SAGLANI Whetstone, North London

Every organisation, country and team has someone in their history who spearheaded much of the success. In America it was Lincoln, at Virgin it is Branson, at Liverpool it was Shankly and at Tottenham Hotspur it is William Edward Nicholson.

An essential part of the 1950-51 Push and Run League championship winning side and the manager behind our Double success ten years later, Bill is quite rightly known as Mr Tottenham. He is fondly regarded by all Spurs fans who will forever be indebted to him.

PAUL BEESON Hainault

Three memories spring into my mind when I think of Bill, all complete contrasts and one of them involves meeting the great man in person.

The first, as a schoolboy, was 1973 at White Hart Lane while waiting for my dad outside the west stand after a game and out walked Bill. I had no pen so couldn't ask for an autograph and all I could think to say was, "I'm gonna play for Spurs one day Bill." He gave me a wry smile and said, "I hope you do son, just as long as you play the Spurs way and wear the badge with pride."

The second was not so happy. It was the night of the 1974 Uefa Cup final, the second leg in Rotterdam and watching the great man so upset and in tears as he appealed for calm.

The third and the saddest of all but in a way pleasing the day I took my sons to the Lane to pay tribute to the great man after he passed away. I took my old scarf and a picture of him to lay on the pitch. My boys took their own tributes, poems they had written. As my eyes filled up I looked around at the people, fellow Spurs fans of all ages, races and both sexes all united in grief but so grateful that he, Sir Bill Nick, had graced our great club as a player, manager, scout, ambassador and fan. What a man

LEANNE BARNES Poole, Dorset

Bill Nicholson - the most successful Tottenham manager of all time! He was completely dedicated to us, the man responsible for bringing the glory, glory days to Tottenham Hotspur. His double winning side of the 60's is the one people still talk about and the one we fans, to this day, want Spurs teams to emulate.

He'll always be remembered for the way he wanted us to play football with style so as to entertain the fans. He lived and breathed Tottenham Hotspur!

AVB will be our next great manager, but in his own way – you simply cannot copy the master. He was inimitable! He was Mr Tottenham Hotspur and will always be regarded by Spurs fans as 'Sir' Bill of Tottenham.

KEVIN FIELD Lincoln

A couple of off-beat recollections of the great Bill Nicholson. The first occurred on 12th April 1971 when Spurs were playing away at Bloomfield Road in Blackpool, when both teams were in the old First Division. Spurs were later than usual arriving at the ground and we, the away fans, were getting rather concerned. Eventually the coach was seen accompanied by a police motor cyclist outrider who was clearing traffic so that the coach could progress safely to the ground. Billy Nick was the first man off the coach and instead of walking into the Away Team entrance, he went to the police officer and shook his hand, thanking him for his assistance. I doubt that many, if in fact any, Premiership managers would take the time to do that today.

The second experience I wish to share is how I obtained his autograph. I was always too shy to approach the great man and when I reached the grand old age of 50 I thought that it was now or never. I trawled the Internet to find his home address and sent a request, thanking him for making Spurs everything it is and asking for his autograph. I enclosed a stamped addressed envelope should he grant my request. By return of post I received a signed short note thanking me for my letter and also a signed photo of him holding the FA Cup. I will never part with these and have added them to my Spurs Collection.

From these two simple actions I can confirm what a true gentleman Billy Nick was, and I would like to publicly thank him for everything he has done to make our club what it is today.

JONATHAN GODDARD Kettering

I always had huge respect for the man and enjoyed the odd occasion in his later years when he was introduced before games with 100% applause coming from the stands, but the poignant time that will always stay with me is the memorial service that was held in his memory with anecdotes from past players such as Chivers, Perryman and Mabbutt, real gut wrenching stuff and you really felt like you had lost one of your own.

JOHN HUNT Barnet

Bill Nicholson was a lovely gentleman – a serene character in later life who seemed to glide around White Hart Lane. My proudest possession is a copy of the Glory Glory Nights, which I get signed by as many Spurs legends as possible. He signed the book for me on the launch night, and when other legends add to the book, they often reflect on the great man. Sadly missed but never forgotten.

SIOBHAN BRUNTON Cheshunt

I had the pleasure of meeting Bill when I worked at Spurs as Ossie and Stevie P's secretary in the early 90's. He used to call me Muscles and went mad if anyone wore red at work! Happy days.

NEIL CARTER Chigwell

I was lucky enough to bump into the great man after a particularly awful evening defeat in the 90's. We were, as many will recall, very poor in the mid 90s. I had just exited the East stand and was walking along Worcester Avenue towards Park Lane when out of the "Corporate" entrance emerged Bill Nicholson, leaning on his walking stick, and he stopped right in front of me. A bit star struck, all I could think to say was "Mr Nicholson, I'm so sorry you had to witness that awful display." He simply smiled, laughed, nodded and said, "Aye, me too!"

ANDY GIRLING, Eltham

In the late 60's when travelling back by train from Sheffield after the game, I saw the Tottenham team all get in the First Class compartments at Sheffield station. After some gentle persuasion from my mate I knocked on the carriage door where Mr. Nicholson was sitting, and politely asked him for his autograph. He gladly obliged and passed the programme around the compartment so that Eddie Baily signed it along with Ray Evans and Mike England. 'Sir Bill' then whispered in my ear and asked me to tell anyone else not to disturb them. I felt so proud and I still have the signed programme as a memento. Happy Days.

STEPHEN VISHNICK London N20

I was 16 when a friend (a fanatical Spurs supporter) of my late father mentioned after two games into the Double winning season that the guy who sat next to him had to relocate his job to Leeds and did I wish to purchase his season ticket. I duly handed over the asking price of 7 guineas and, of course the rest is Glorious footballing history. Never was 7 guineas better spent!

Nothing can erase or eclipse the memory of Danny, Dave, John White, Cliffie JonesJones etc, and I am sure these heroes would not look out of place in the Premier league today.

My greatest game memory was the night we played Eusebio-enriched Benfica at home. We won but lost on goal difference. Having also lost my voice I expressed my disappoint in silent gestures.

Football and the people in it have changed but those Glory Glory days will stay with me forever and just to mention that the sight of Jimmy Greaves rounding a keeper will keep me going into old age. And all down to the great Bill Nicholson.

MARY CUMNER-PRICE Cheshunt

Bill Nicholson was a great man, who never changed. He knew who he was and where he came from. My late husband was headmaster of a North London school and was inspirational to thousands of pupils (as well as persuading them to support Spurs rather than that other team). Andrew, one of our three Spurs-mad sons, was at university when his father became ill and wanted to give up. His father took a leaf out of Bill Nick's book and told him: 'Never be a quitter.' Andrew went on to get an MA and I am very proud of him, as he will discover when he reads this book!

KEITH ANDREW Chelmsford

My father was manager of a butchers shop opposite the White Hart Lane ground in the 1950s, and many of the players called in to buy meat. I was off school and working in the shop with my father when Bill came in and I had the chance to speak with him.

We chatted about the team, which of course included at that time legends like Alf Ramsey, and Eddie Baily. I told him that I was a regular attendee and that I watched most games from what was still then a boys only enclosure, from where we used to lob apple cores and other missiles at the coppers around the pitch.

He asked if I would like to watch a game from the stands, which of course I said I would and sure enough he delivered two tickets for me and my brother to see a game. We felt like the bees knees and lived off that for years after.

My sports teacher, also a Spurs fan, was very jealous, so much so that he arranged for our football team to get entrance and we were allowed to walk onto the ground via the players' tunnel and sit on the touchline. The only disappointment was that we lost to the Arsenal that day!

Bill was a real gent and both a great player and manager. I feel privileged to have seen him play and meet him.

ASHLEY COLLIE California:

Having been brought up in South Wales, home to 4th Division Newport County, I was a long way removed on the M4 from the First Division and White Hart Lane. So I only got to see Spurs players when the home international games were contested at Cardiff. As a nipper, I met Greavsie there once outside the ground and got his autograph. But I also saw other Lilywhites like Cliff Jones, Dave Mackay, Bill Brown … and guys on my dad's team like Bestie, Charlton and Law.

But the first time I saw Spurs live was actually in Canada after we emigrated from Wales. Spurs were playing Rangers in the Toronto Cup at Varsity Stadium — where much later on two of my soon to be Canadian-born brothers both played their Canadian collegiate championship games for the University of Toronto. (I also saw Pele, Michel Platini, other visiting stars and NASL games at Varsity.)

June 1, 1969 – couldn't believe it, we'd emigrated and Spurs actually came to Toronto. There wasn't much security around those days. My dad passed himself off as a photographer and we got close to the action. Greavsie scored a hat-trick that day, and we beat Rangers 4-3. When the team and Billy Nick came out at half-time, I

SCRAPBOOK MEMORIES: The changing of the guard., 1954. Danny Blanchflower arrives to take over from Bill Nick in the No 4 Spurs shirt. Alf Ramsey departs to start a managerial career at Ipswich.

got a photo with my hero Greavsie and another autograph on the programme. My dad said something complimentary to Billy Nick about Greavsie and the legend responded, "He is some player!" That was it. The greatest day of my life...until I later returned to see Spurs at Wembley and finally at WHL! Billy Nick sold my hero the following year in 1970 to West Ham!

ROBERT ROCKETT Cookham, Berks

I met Sir Bill at the Haringey Irish Centre a few years back when he and his charming wife Darkie visited. They were a wonderful couple. I first started watching Tottenham in the late 60's, my first match was at home to Liverpool. In those days Bill made Tottenham a hard team to beat at home albeit on a mudheap of a pitch. Such memories of a great team inspired by Mr Tottenham.

DICKIE BALDWIN Tottenham

I was born in Tottenham, 1965, to a family of Spurs fans and started going to the Lane regularly in the 1974/75 season when the team was under the guidance of Terry Neill, so only just missed the Bill Nicholson era. However I'm told I was taken to a game in the late 60's, up on my Grandad's shoulders.

These were the days when you could walk through the old wooden light blue doors in Paxton Road for the second-half for free. Apparently we went in to meet my Dad, I cried and had to leave. BUT, I am proud to say I 'saw' a game with Bill Nicholson as manager! That's something my current group of friends/season ticket holders can't say (apart from a few of the older ones).

I was given a load of Spurs handbooks from the 50's & 60's that my my Mum picked up at a jumble sale at about the same time I became a regular, and I read them back to front constantly. I was a pretty well-read Spurs historian before my teenage years (and still am) so was always in awe of the great man.

I had the pleasure of meeting him twice, once in the legends bar after a game in the early 90's and then again in 2002 when I had my picture taken with him.

Without wanting to name drop I have had privilege of having

met Steve Perryman on a number of occasions who speaks so highly of his Boss and told so many great stories it would make your hair stand on end. Also Cliff Jones ,who I managed to 'corner' after he spoke at my football club dinner, telling the story of his meeting with the manager, asking for a wage rise as the press had started calling him the 'best winger in the world'.

The famous answer is true: "That's their opinion. Not mine. And it's mine that counts. Now get out."

Fantastic! Imagine that happening now? The main thing that comes through is his total decency and pure honesty. Unfortunately we'll never see his type down here again, but as long as people who knew him keep spreading his good word then our proud history and style will carry on.

SEÁN HURL Winchester

Looking back from an era of rent-a-quote coaches to when, in 1967, I fell in love with football, and Tottenham Hotspur Football Club in particular, I think of Bill Nicholson as a humble man of few words but he knew implicitly how the game should be played, both in spirit and style. A stern man to his players, when he did speak it was common sense, passionate, wise and worth listening to. He was the essence of the Club, he set the standards that I, as a fan, have come to expect of the Mighty Spurs.

SHAUN BOYLE ex-Midlands now in Mallorca

My special memory of Bill Nicholson goes back to the mid-1970s. Dismissed and, at the time, quietly discarded from the club he had dedicated his life to with extraordinary success, some friends and I, mostly based in the Midlands, decided to play a couple of games of football to raise some money and get him a 'thank you' gift. The dates and details are fading with time, but we got our gift and made contact with Mr. Nicholson. We assembled in the shadow of the White Hart Lane stadium at the pub on the corner and waited.

As it wasn't a match day, that night seemed so different and somehow sad. To add to the dismal mood it was raining. Friends

Tony and Irene, who were neighbours of the Nicholsons, went to tell Mr. Nicholson and his lovely wife, Darky, we had arrived. They were never pretentious and lived in a modest house close to the ground.

I anticipated a rather sad evening, but Mr. Nicholson – he insisted on us all calling him Bill – was having none of it. He arrived with his wife, both of them immaculately dressed, he in his trademark smart suit and she in a beautiful coat.

He escorted his wife to a seat and she chatted amongst us, while he held court.

"You are a lucky bunch of lads," he said "This is the first time I've been to a pub round here for 20 years!"

He looked at Tom, a towering member of our assembly. "You should get a trial. At six foot five, you've got the makings of a centre-half."

Mr. Nicholson, sorry, Bill, was in good spirits, thanking us one by one for coming all that way from the Midlands.

I made a short presentation speech, choking on my words, and as he accepted an engraved silver plate he said: "Who's got the camera?"

In the frenzy nobody had remembered to bring one. But it didn't matter. The picture of the moment was frozen into our minds for ever. The only thing that mattered was that we were there and we did it. The local newspaper reported that we had given Mr. Nicholson a bigger send-off than the club. I have been proud to be a Tottenham supporter for 50 years and that evening I met a great man.

KEITH ANDREW Chelmsford

My father was manager of a butchers shop opposite the White Hart Lane ground in the 1950s, and many of the players called in to buy meat. I was off school and working in the shop with my father when Bill came in and I had the chance to speak with him. We chatted about the team, which of course included at that time legends like Alf Ramsey, and Eddie Baily. I told him that I was a regular attendee and that I watched most games from what was still then a boys only enclosure from where we used to lob apple cores and other missiles at the coppers around the pitch.

He asked if I would like to watch a game from the stands, which of course I said I would and sure enough he delivered two tickets for me and my brother to see a game and we felt like the bees knees and lived off that for years after.

My sports teacher who was also a Spurs fan was very jealous, so much so that he arranged for our football team to get entrance and were were allowed to walk onto the ground via the players' tunnel and sit on the touchline. The only disappointment was that we lost the Arsenal that day! Bill was a real gent and both a great player and manager and I feel privileged to have seen him play and met him.

VIC POWER, Saffron Walden, Essex

Football memories differ from most others. I'm not sure why but they touch a part of us that is unique. I mean why should we care about the fate of people we don't know? why do we share their joys and miseries? That's what football does to us so when we tap into the memory bank and withdraw a football memory, it is different, it evokes an almost mystical feeling which stays with us for life.

It's fairly universally true that we support the same team as our dads although with more women watching football these days it may well be our mum. So it was with me, my dad was a Spurs fan and there could be no other team for me.

Before I was deemed old enough to visit the shrine at White Hart Lane I would hear of names like Tommy Harmer, Len Douquemin, George Robb and the like. I ached to see them in person but it wasn't my time yet. There was to be another arrival at the Lane before I was to make my first visit.

It was Saturday October 11th 1958 and it was an eventful day. Firstly because my dad was to be taken shopping rather than be allowed to 'go down the Spurs' and secondly, Bill Nicholson was appointed manager for his first game against Everton.

As an eight year old, I was excused shopping and was dropped off at my grandparents Hackney council flat whilst the shopping torture took place with firm instructions to make sure I heard the results, or rather the result as Spurs was the only game that mattered. I duly obliged and sat in front of the telly to watch another debut. October 11th 1958 was not only the debut of my dad going shopping and Billy Nick managing Spurs, it was the first airing of Grandstand.

The clipped tones of Peter Dimmock waffled on about the sports action of the day but there was one match that stood out from the rest. The results were read:

"Tottenham Hotspur ten" (upward inflection followed by slight pause) … "Everton four" (downward inflection). What? Ten-four? Ten bloody four? Broderick Crawford eat your heart out!

Minutes later a breathless dad rat tat tatted on the door and nan let him in followed by a bag-laden mum. Years later I may have teased him a little but as an eight year old I lacked the finesse for a wind-up, so I excitedly blurted the score. "Stop messing about what was the score?" It took four or five attempts to get him to believe me.

Then the realisation dawned. He had spent the last four hours traipsing round Ridley Road market and up and down Mare Street and had missed this earth shattering event. The look he gave mum will stay with me even though she was so pleased with the new loo brush.

If I didn't know before, I knew now that Spurs would be the only team for me and I'd never put a loo brush before the white shirt and cockerel.

ROGER PITT Malvern

I would like to contribute some thoughts from a Wolves perspective. We had been trying for the elusive double and but for a suspect result in Lancashire we would have achieved it in season 59-60. It would also have been our third Championship in a row. The very next season the famous Spurs team did obtain the double and I thought any man who could succeed where Stan Cullis had failed must be some kind of manager. Bill Nick was that man.

I offer two further thoughts. His team played football the right way and ever since then it is as if all Spurs teams must try and do the same to keep his name alive. Finally apart from any Wolves team and the boys of 66 that Spurs team is the only one where I can go from 1 to 11 without thinking. After 52 years that speaks volumes about that team and that manager!

PAUL SMITH www.spursodyssey.com

On Saturday 23rd October 2004 I received the news of the passing of the greatest man in Spurs history with deep, deep regret. I can find no words to describe "Sir Bill" better than those of Daniel Levy in the programme for the induction of Bill into the Spurs Hall of Fame. Bill Nicholson was the Rock upon which Tottenham Hotspur, as we know it today, was built. He will always be revered in that fashion. The World, Football, and Tottenham Hotspur lost a great man indeed.

I think especially of Bill's loving wife (the late "Darkie") all his family, contemporaries, and those players who had the honour of playing for Bill, especially those surviving members of the Double team who were also installed into the Spurs Hall of Fame.

Bill Nicholson was a part of Tottenham Hotspur since he was signed as a player way back in 1938. His loyalty to one club through thick and thin knew no bounds. "Sir" Bill's benign, smiling, spiritual presence will shine over all at Tottenham for evermore.

God Bless "Mr Tottenham". I still miss him. I feel like I have lost a dear member of my family.

STEVE HAYWARD Houghton Regis, Beds

Having supported Spurs all my life, and coming from Tottenham obviously Bill Nicholson was like a god to me. I work for Openreach, BT as they were called around 1990, and at that time I sometimes had jobs at White Hart Lane. One particular day, I was getting some equipment out of my van in the car park, and I saw a grey Ford Granada drive past me and back into a parking space. I then heard a thud. On looking over to see what had happened, I saw that the car had backed up and just caught a bollard. I then noticed that it was Bill Nicholson. He looked at me sheepishly and said "Don`t tell anyone will you". "Of course not Mr Nicholson," I replied and smiled. The funny thing was he seemed surprised that I knew who he was, which somehow caught the modesty of the great man.

It was just a brief moment, but something I`ll never forget. Mr Tottenham, the legend and should have been Sir Bill Nicholson actually spoke to me! These days I am a matchday Steward at Spurs, I have done this for 23 years as well as being a BT engineer. Everytime I go to the ground, the Park Lane End, I feel the presence of our greatest ever manager. SIr Bill Nick.

STEVE DUTTON Swanscombe, Kent

Bill was a genious and a gentlemen, a man who could stand as an equal to Shankly. I will never forget his passing, it was a sad day not just for a Spurs fan, but a sad day for football. Myself and my daughter went to White Hart Lane to show our respects to a great man when the doors were open for the fans. It felt like someone in my family had passed. I sat next to the pitch in silence and recalled the Bill Nicholson testimonial, when Bill walked onto the pitch he was given a standing ovation which lasted around 10 minutes maybe more. When I think of Bill I think of that night with a lump in my throat and tears in my eyes. Players, managers etc are given the name "legend" too easily now, but Billy Nick was a legend.

LEON RUSKIN Ross on Wye, Herefordshire

I was lucky enough to watch Bill as a nuggety wing-half (as they were then called) who could also play centre or fullback. Without being spectacular, he fulfilled the exact need we had then. He played in front of a meticulous right back, Alf Ramsey (later knighted, of course, for managing England's only World Cup victory), a slow, precise footballer, for whom Nicholson as a perfect complement, covering any gaps in defence.

At the same time he also counterbalanced the magnificent dynamo in the team, skipper Ron Burgess. The Welsh powerhouse would tread on every blade of grass over the 90 minutes, and Billy Nick made sure he was always well covered. Bill deserved more than his solitary cap against Portugal, in which he scored with his first touch. However, England were well endowed at that time in his position, including the England skipper, Billy Wright.

Our genius manager, Arthur Rowe, recognised Nicholson's post-playing potential as coach and manager, and when he took over as manager in October 1958, it was soon obvious that here was a manager extraordinary. Within a few years he had achieved the seemingly impossible prize of a Cup and League double with the talent he assembled.

His business dealings were always exemplary, and I believe this cost him further laurels as soccer ethics generally declined. I recall being with Michael Parkinson when we heard the news that Nicholson had retired. Parky was almost tearful as he mourned the loss to soccer of one of its greatest ever managers, a true gent who was "straight as a pole."

Parky attributed his early departure to the fighting that was marring the game, and the low standards of ethics. A true Spurs legend.

GARY WRIGHT Ilford

I never met Bill but can always remember the TV camera picking out his face in the stand. I don't think they ever caught a smile, rather an intense look as he was about his work as his players tried to meet his high expectations on the pitch.

I remember listening to Bill on a radio interview on Sports Report as I travelled back from another blistering Spurs win. Well blistering for us fans but for Bill there was always more that could be done or an ingredient that could be added.

In his Yorkshire accent and rather soft tones he explained that it was the goals that were missed that worried him not the seven that had been scored.

His ideals of football were set high and his expectations of his beloved Spurs even higher. For Bill the next goal was always the most important and this was a life lesson we all could learn from.

Like a loved Uncle Bill was always a person you gave respect and that you listened to what he said. I expect his players must have felt the same as he put greatness at the beginning of their names and why he was one of the greatest ever football managers and why he is still cherished by ex-players and Spurs fans.

TONY LEACH Egerton, Kent

The day I watched the very first "The Big Match" on ITV as a wide-eyed nine-year-old, I was totally captivated by the Spurs side playing fast, sweeping football against my team, Charlton, and enthused over by the authoritative commentary of the untouchable Brian Moore, a fellow Man of Kent.

Pat Jennings arching back and catching a looping cross one handed and languidly kicking the ball up to the balding yet agile Gilzean to flick on to the dancing feet of a beautifully balanced, composed Greavsie to dash past two defenders before passing the ball into the net with such aplomb I swear that was the moment that stayed with me throughout my forthcoming schoolboy football career.

After the game ended and following the commercial break I remember seeing this middle-aged gruff-sounding northern bloke briefly being asked about his team's performance, and he didn't seem particularly overjoyed.

Slightly confused I turned to my dad, who told me that was Bill Nicholson, the Spurs manager, who'd been with the club for ages and was a great manager.

To my young brain how could this boring old bloke have anything to do with what I saw in this all-consuming football being played to feet at pace with control and movement and composure the like of which I rarely witnessed at The Valley.

It was only as I grew up and collected snippets of the life and remarkable managerial career of Billy Nick that I finally grasped the importance and unconditional reverence in which he was rightly held by the club and supporters.

It is one of life's enduring mysteries of injustice that he was never invited to become a Knight of the Realm.

THE last word from the supporters goes to Davie Elder, who is collecting a huge following on line as The Spurs Poet:

DAVIE 'The Spurs Poet' ELDER County Tyrone

The final whistle sounds
as the players leave the ground
Fans have all made their way
to journeys homeward bound

And as the floodlights get switched off
a darkness does descend
But Tottenham does not go to sleep
the history does not end

The ground is deadly quiet
but a presence still is there
The stands are all so empty
but there's an echo in the air

It is better to fail aiming high
than to succeed aiming low
The words of a great man
one we all should know

His name was Bill Nicholson
he was Tottenham to his core
He loved this famous football club
whose tops we have all wore

He said "It's no use just winning,
we've got to win it well."
a famous line to his players
that Sir Bill Nick would tell

As a player and a manager
he was dedicated to our team
Push and Run with Arthur Rowe
was Nicholson's Tottenham dream

And with just one cap for England
and a goal that he did score
Injuries badly plagued him,
For St George he played no more

"My duty is to get fit for Tottenham.
Well, they pay my wages you see"
Words of a true loyal man
not a modern day mercenary

But his playing career was over
his future was laid out
He got his life ambition
and his name we all did shout

He rewrote the history books
with his style and passing play
people wanted to learn
all about the Tottenham way

We went on to win the Double
in the year of 61
Tottenham Hotspur football club's
new era had begun

Trophies and glory followed
we'd conquered the English game
Then he moved to Europe
to share the new found fame

First team to do the Double
and first to beat Europe's elite
Bill had transformed us
to the team they craved to beat

BILL NICHOLSON REVISITED

He'd made the club a world wide name
and history books rewrote
He gave the club the stature
and was famous for a quote

When he left he must have thought
his job he must have done
But he came back for Burkinshaw
and the transformation again begun

He scouted for the team he loved
and players he did find
Galvin, Mabbut and Roberts
are a few that spring to mind

He received the tribute he deserved
for what he had achieved
Club president to the day
we were so sadly bereaved

A dark day for Tottenham
on October 23rd 2004
When the great man passed away,
a man we will forever adore

A legend in his own right
and a true Tottenham great
The day he died the club had mourned
that devastating date

So when the lights are turned off
the legend's still alive
He loved the club with passion
it helped the great man thrive

And as his ashes are scattered
on the turf at White Hart Lane
You have got to show his passion
when you play the football game

So every player at Tottenham
remember where you are
Remember when you leave
with big wages and nice car

You will always be a number
and a name for Spurs to pick
You will never be a legend
like the legend that was Bill Nick

203

Final Shots
The Master of the Lane

IF Bill Nicholson has come out of this book seeming anything less than a good man and an exceptional manager, then I have failed in my mission to write the definitive study of the Master of White Hart Lane. Cynical critics will no doubt say it is not warts 'n' all, but when I paint a word portrait I like to capture the best in people, and you would have to look hard to find any blemishes on Bill Nick.

Yes, he was mean and miserly with his praise of players, but that was because he never wanted them to feel self satisfied. That breeds complacency. Bill was like a dedicated mountaineer who always had higher peaks to scale; an ultra perfectionist, and if that must be counted in the warts category then he can be accused of having been too demanding.

A clue to his character is that having been brought up in a large family in Scarborough during the Depression years, he expected and demanded little out of life, and was more than somewhat surprised by what he eventually achieved. He could never come to terms with players wanting praise for doing their job. He often used to say to his team: "That's what you're paid for. That's what the public expect, and they are the ones who pay your wages. They work hard for their entrance money, and they want your total commitment in return."

Harsh? Possibly. True? Definitely. It was an outlook that epitomised Bill's startling honesty. He would not countenance or tolerate cheating or giving anything less than 100 per cent.

I spent hours in his company and can never recall him once falling below the high standards of behaviour he had set for himself, and expected of his players.

He was not a laugh-a-minute companion, but drill through the serious shield behind which he guarded his shy nature and you found a genuine, generous and gilt-edged gentleman.

Only Bill could have regarded the greatest day in Tottenham's history as a flat, frustrating occasion. When Spurs completed the historic Double by beating Leicester City 2-0 in the FA Cup final at Wembley he was disappointed, because it was a victory that was chiselled out rather than performed with a flourish, or in Bill's words "the Spurs way." He always wanted victory in style.

Tottenham eventually got round to giving him two testimonial matches, but they came late in his life and in my opinion did not begin to make up for the fact that throughout his managerial career he was appallingly underpaid.

It did not bother Bill. But it should surely have bothered the consciences of the men who allowed him to give blood, sweat and tears for the club that he, more than anybody, put on the football map. He deserved much better treatment.

If Bill was around to read this he would tell me: "You're writing fairy stories again. Stick to the facts."

The facts are that Bill Nicholson represented the soul and the spirit of Spurs. He sacrificed much of his social and family life to give all his time and energy to his second family at White Hart Lane. His beloved wife, Darkie, had to share him with Spurs.

Those of us who knew him well saw him mellow once he had escaped the extreme pressure of management. It was as if a huge weight had been lifted off his shoulders, and he was able to relax and take a fresh look at the game and the club that he loved. He was happy to take a back seat on his return to Tottenham, never interfering but as keen as ever to see Spurs playing with the style, the skill and the invention that had marked his reign.

His passing in 2004 caused widespread grief, and the football world came together to remember with warmth and respect one of the finest servants the game has ever known.

Tottenham honoured him with a bust, but I hope that – when the new Spurs stadium is eventually built – they erect a larger-than-life statue to remind future generations of the debt they owe the man who laid the foundation to their club.

Bill Nicholson, the Master of White Hart Lane.

PREVIOUS BOOKS BY NORMAN GILLER

Lane of Dreams (introduced by Jimmy Greaves and Steve Perryman)

Tottenham, The Managing Game

The Glory Glory Game (Spurs Writers' Club) **The Golden Double**

Jimmy Greaves At Seventy (with Michael Giller and Terry Baker)

Banks of England (with Gordon Banks) **Footballing Fifties**

The Glory and the Grief (with George Graham)

Banks v Pelé (with Terry Baker)

Football And All That   **Bobby Moore The Master**

The Seventies Revisited (with Kevin Keegan)

The Final Score (with Brian Moore)

ABC of Soccer Sense (with Tommy Docherty)

Billy Wright, A Hero for All Seasons (official biography)

The Rat Race (with Tommy Docherty)

Denis Compton (The Untold Stories)

McFootball, the Scottish Heroes of the English Game

The Book of Rugby Lists (with Gareth Edwards)

The Book of Tennis Lists (with John Newcombe)

The Book of Golf Lists   **TV Quiz Trivia**   **Sports Quiz Trivia**

Know What I Mean (with Frank Bruno)

Eye of the Tiger (with Frank Bruno)

From Zero to Hero (with Frank Bruno)

 The Judge Book of Sports Answers

Watt's My Name (with Jim Watt)

My Most Memorable Fights (with Henry Cooper)

How to Box (with Henry Cooper)

Henry Cooper's 100 Greatest Boxers

Henry Cooper A Hero for All Time

Mike Tyson Biography

Mike Tyson, the Release of Power (with Reg Gutteridge)

Crown of Thorns, the World Heavyweight Title (with Neil Duncanson)
Fighting for Peace (Barry McGuigan biography, with Peter Batt)

World's Greatest Cricket Matches/World's Greatest Football Matches

Golden Heroes (with Dennis Signy) **The Judge** (1,001 Q&A)

The Great Football IQ Quiz Book (The Judge of The Sun)

The Marathon Kings The Golden Milers (with Sir Roger Bannister) **Olympic Heroes** (with Brendan Foster)

Olympics Handbook 1980   Olympics Handbook 1984

Book of Cricket Lists (with Tom Graveney)

Top Ten Cricket Book (with Tom Graveney)

Cricket Heroes (with Eric Morecambe)   **Big Fight Quiz Book**

TVIQ Puzzle Book   Lucky the Fox (with Barbara Wright)

Gloria Hunniford's TV Challenge

Chopper's Chelsea (with Ron Harris)

Hammers '80 (with Sir Trevor Brooking)

Concorde Club (First 50 years)   **Keys to Paradise** (with Jeni Robbins)

Comedy novels:

Carry On Doctor Carry On England Carry On Loving

Carry On Up the Khyber Carry On Abroad   Carry On Henry

What A Carry On

Satzenbrau-sponsored **Sports Puzzle Book** and **TV Puzzle Book**

A Stolen Life (novel) **Mike Baldwin: Mr Heartbreak** (novel)
Hitler's Final Victim (novel) **Affairs** (novel) **The Bung** (novel)

The Glory and the Greed (novel)

Books in collaboration with RICKY TOMLINSON

Football My Arse/Celebrities My Arse/Cheers My Arse

Reading My Arse (The Search for the Rock Island Line)

PLUS books in collaboration with JIMMY GREAVES:

This One's On Me The Final (novel) **The Ball Game (**novel)

The Boss (novel) **The Second Half** (novel) **Let's Be Honest** (with Reg Gutteridge) **Greavsie's Heroes and Entertainers**

World Cup History   GOALS!   Stop the Game, I Want to Get On

Book of Football Lists Taking Sides   Sports Quiz Challenge

Sports Quiz Challenge 2 It's A Funny Old Life Saint & Greavsie's 1990 World Cup Special   The Sixties Revisited   Don't Shoot the Manager Funny Old Games (with the Saint) **Greavsie's Greatest**

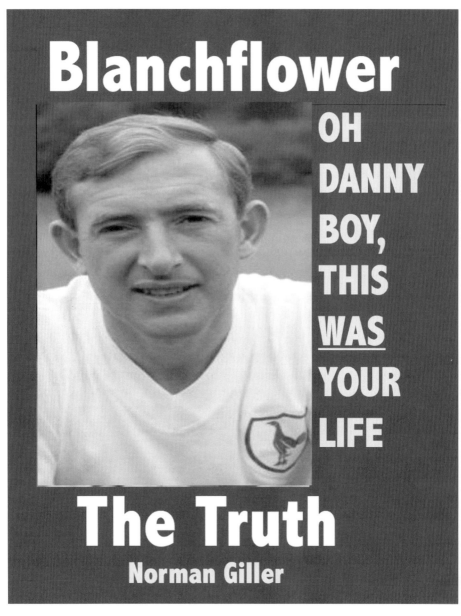

Blanchflower

OH DANNY BOY, THIS <u>WAS</u> YOUR LIFE

The Truth

Norman Giller

The NEXT book from the pen of Norman Giller.
Publication: Spring 2014
For details please email: author@normangillerbooks.com